Praise for
When Your Parents Sign the Paychecks

"An outstanding step-by-step roadmap for avoiding a major pitfall in the perpetuation of family business: an unqualified and unprepared younger generation."

Steve Swartz, Pioneer in Family Business Consulting and
Former President of the Family Firm Institute

"I urge you to read this pragmatic and thoughtful book as a critical investment in yourself, your next generation, and your family business."

Dr. Pramodita Sharma, Professor of Management and Associate Dean
at the School of Business & Economics, Wilfrid Laurier University, and
Associate Editor for The Family Business Review

"Challenging and inspirational...for passive successors who feel that the family business will carry them through life with little or no effort."

Chris Johnston, Chairman, J & AG Johnston Ltd.,
the oldest known family business in South Australia

"Captures the essence of the challenges faced by the next generation… Provides insightful methods to achieve personal and professional success."

Ann Kinkade, Director of the Family Business Center and
Faculty Associate, University of Wisconsin-Madison

"Implementing the concepts in this book can truly be life changing--making a family closer and helping the family business beat the odds of transitioning control from generation to the next."

Jill Shipley, MBA, Innovation & Learning Center at
Asset Management Advisors, and Stetson University
Family Business Graduate

"Essential for any student considering entering the family's business."

Shannon McFarland, next generation of a family that owns a business
and Stetson University Family Business Graduate

When Your
Parents
Sign the
Paychecks

FINDING CAREER SUCCESS INSIDE OR OUTSIDE THE FAMILY BUSINESS

GREG McCANN

ISBN-13:978-1484187012
ISBN-10:1484187016

McCann & Associates 2013
DeLand, FL

www.gregmccannspeaks.com

Use This Book to Start on Your Own Career Path

Have you written down goals for your life and career? If you're like most people, you haven't. That's unfortunate because setting goals is a major factor in being successful. You may be seduced into thinking that because your family owns a business that you don't need to put much effort into making a career plan. After all, you can always get a job with the family business, right? But the path to happiness and career success is to find a career that aligns with who you are and what you want, and you might not find this career in your family's business.

As a member of a business-owning family, you have opportunities that many other people don't have. However, you also face challenges that other people don't face. This book will help you to make the most of the opportunities and confront the challenges. This book can help you reshape your vision of yourself, your family, your family's business, and your future, thus empowering you and motivating you to pursue a course of action that will improve your chances of success. The key factors in this are to improve your credibility and establish marketability.

If you are ready to take ownership for your life and write your own script, then let this book be your guide.

Dedication

*To my loving, caring, and wise parents,
Rosemary and Norm McCann.*

Acknowledgements

As I write this, Stetson University's Family Enterprise Center is about to celebrate its fifteenth anniversary. As its founder and director, creating this book has been an important part of my experience at the center, and it epitomizes my commitment to the next generation. It also reflects the Family Enterprise Center's innovative approach toward education, using a broader, more holistic process we call *development*. This holistic development process calls on us to not only address the nuts and bolts of accounting, finance, marketing and management, but to remember that a human being is at the center of those subjects and include that realization in the equation.

I believe this book strives to do that, too, and feedback from clients has been encouraging. I recall one 89-year old matriarch telling me she liked this book "because it is about character not money." So other clients have requested we incorporate this book and its principles into our work with their next generation, and that has been very validating: There is no test like the marketplace of ideas to see if your own have merit.

This book would not have occurred, nor would this edition have happened without the support, generosity, and time of dear friends and talented colleagues, Norm McCann, Jill Shipley, Michelle DeMoss, and Steve Swartz. Their faith in me is far more unwavering than seems warranted. Likewise, my patient and talented editor-cum-writing coach, Morris Sullivan, helped me craft this book into something accessible yet rich in content. I believe this edition shows our intention toward ongoing improvement.

As the second edition goes to print, I would be remiss if I didn't mention Audra Jolliffe, my trusted colleague who has managed all the parts of this endeavor, and a diligent Family Enterprise Major, Emily Dudley, who helped us with the revisions. Both were invaluable in managing the details that are necessary to such an effort.

I have been grateful for the Family Enterprise students who have used the book and given me feedback, as well as teachers from other universities who did likewise. Finally I would like to thank Stetson University, especially the current dean, Dr. Tom Schwarz, for his support not only with this book but in my efforts to bring innovation to the field of family enterprise.

CONTENTS

CONTENTS

CONTENTS

Foreword

So your family owns a business? You are not alone. More than half of our nation's GDP (Gross Domestic Product) is produced by families that own businesses. And family-owned businesses are not all small businesses. According to a University of Southern Maine study published by *Business Week* in February 2006, family businesses make up 35 percent of the S&P 500. Household names like Ford Motor Company, Anheuser-Busch, Wal-Mart, and Publix are all family businesses.

Yet families that own businesses face unique challenges that threaten to jeopardize not only the business's success, but also the family's harmony. The two major transitions that families and businesses face are especially challenging, and they often occur at the same time for families that own businesses. The kids go off to college, and the business faces a succession in leadership and possibly ownership. Managed correctly, these transitions can create tremendous value for the individuals, families, and businesses involved. The tragedy lies in how seldom family businesses actively talk about, reflect on, and plan for these transitions.

This book will help you navigate those potential pitfalls and avoid the misfortune that causes two-thirds of the nation's family businesses to fail after each generation. Dr. Greg McCann has not only worked with his family's businesses, but he also has consulted for numerous other families' businesses. On top of that, he has studied, researched, and taught on the topic at the university level for the past nine years. Having helped to found and shape Stetson University's Family Business Center, Dr. McCann has dedicated his efforts to the next generation of family business employees, advisors, and owners. If you are entering college coming from a family that owns a business, there is no better guide available today. Even if you are a parent sending a child off to college as a family business owner, this book can apply in a unique way to you. You see, there's a key to effectively managing any transition, family business or otherwise. It's a two-way street, and both parties have to be equally well informed in order to understand the other's position.

We represent that two-way street. As a son who went to college trying to find his future and a father who owns a CPA (Certified Public Accounting) firm, the dialogue Dr. McCann helped us create as a family proved more valuable than any other experience at the university.

As the son entering college, I met Dr. McCann my first day on Stetson's campus. As Dad and I were unpacking my belongings, he told me that he had set up a meeting with one of the professors he knew, the Director of the Family Business Center. I immediately thought, "Here we go again! Dad is trying to set me up with someone he knows to get ahead, instead of letting me do it myself." Regardless of his intentions, I came to realize how dead wrong—and yet truthful—my first reaction had been. My dad was trying to introduce me to a professor so I could get a head start, but I would end up doing the work myself. Dr. McCann made sure of that.

Over the course of the next four years, through countless hours of self-reflection, soul searching, and personal research, I got my head start. Five formal courses and two internships later, I knew who I was, what I valued, and what career path I wanted to pursue. Beyond that, I had created a portfolio that explained my skills, credentials, and experiences to potential employers. And I did not do this alone. At each step along the way, I was in dialogue with my family. Whether the topic was next semester's course schedule or my decision not to be an accountant, I discussed it with my family. That's what this book is all about: Finding out who you are and what you value and, armed with that knowledge, making conscious choices about your career. In the end, because of my deep self-awareness, I turned down two potentially very lucrative job offers in favor of a company that better fit who I was, what I valued, and what I wanted in an employer. I hope you get the same out of your college experience. If you haven't, this book will go a long way toward filling in the gaps.

As the father sending his son to college, I learned of Dr. McCann's program when he visited my office to explain his education model, which was foursquare with the approach I was taking in dealing with family business transitions that my clients were facing. The only difference was I was usually dealing with these transition situations as they were happening instead of spending time in advance planning and educating the family for the transition. The idea of an educational program in college that reached out to the parents as well as the students was radical, which is why I recommended it to my son.

As a practicing CPA, I serve many of my clients as a business advisor much more than a number cruncher. In filling that role, I am often called upon to deal with family issues, both within the business and the family itself. Advising a businessman about how to treat his family by transitioning management, ownership, and control to the next generation requires much more than knowledge of the income tax code or generally accepted accounting principles. My own life experiences were my primary source of knowledge about how to do this type of consulting. Through the Family Business Center at Stetson and the processes covered in this book, Dr. McCann has provided a major step ahead in the body of knowledge available to family business owners, their successors, and their advisors.

It may seem at first glance that we do not represent the textbook example of a successful family business transition. After all, the son decided not to enter the family's business. But that is not the point of this book. This book is not intended to provide the road map for families to automatically transition their children into their businesses. On the contrary, this book is intended to help the next generation of family business leaders figure out who they really are, what they value, and if entering their family's business benefits them.

As a result, parents who hire their young adult children into their business will no longer be doing an act of charity. The decision will be a well thought-out and well planned-for transition that benefits the family as well as the business. It will be a value-added transition for the parents as well as the children, and it will truly be the best thing for the newly hired young adult. If joining the family business does not align with what's best for the son or daughter, then that decision will also have been actively made. After all, when both the family and its business are involved in this decision, it's a two-way street. There is no greater lesson for a business-owning family.

Trevor R. Whitley, Financial Advisor (and Steven's son) and Steven R. Whitley, C.P.A. (and Trevor's dad)

Introduction

I grew up in a family that has owned businesses for as long as I have been alive. I started working in the family business at age 11 for the whopping salary of $1 a day. Fortunately, my pay rate has gone up a bit over the years, but some things have remained the same. Growing up in such a family gave me important values, including a strong work ethic, a sense of responsibility, and a sense of ownership for my life.

If you are reading this introduction, you have probably grown up in a family that owns a business, and you probably see both the upsides and the challenges. You may enjoy the shared passion for the family enterprise, the greater wealth, and the increased opportunities. At the same time, you may see the additional stress on the family, the greater challenge of separating family matters from business, and the notion that often everything the family has is at risk. These things include money, property, time and effort, and most of all, relationships.

Growing up in such a family, your personal life and your career choices are likely to be more connected, connected in a way far different than if your parents were police officers or college professors. So what are the ramifications when your family owns a business? How do you navigate the different roles you have to play as a family member, as a potential employee in the family's business, and as a potential heir to or owner of the company? Do you have to figure it all out on your own? No, you don't.

How This Book Can Help

This book can help you make an informed career choice. I've based this book on three parts of my life. First, it is based on my experiences working with my family's businesses for more than 35 years. Second, ideas in this book come from my consulting work with businesses in general, but mostly on my consulting work with family businesses since 1999. The biggest influence on this book, however, is my work at Stetson University, where I have been a faculty member since 1990.

In 1998, I became Director of the Family Business Center at the university, where I led the effort to develop the second minor and first major in family business in the United States. I work almost daily with members of the next generation from families that own businesses. I help them both in and out of the classroom, lead retreats and conferences with them and their families, and write about their relationship to the family business. As you read this book, you may see your life differently in terms of what it means to come from a family that owns a business.

This book is not meant to be a study of family business, although there are some very good books available on that topic. (I suggest Dennis Jaffe's *Working with the Ones You Love* or Ernesto Poza's *Family Business*.) Like the program at Stetson University, this book is about the practice of family business. When I talk with groups of family businesses, I'll ask the audience, "If I told you my family and I go away to a gym for one day a year and work out, and that keeps us in shape, would you believe me?" At best, one might think I'm a little deluded; no one can get in shape working out just one day a year. Similarly, the information in this book needs to be applied on an ongoing basis, which is why each chapter is designed to get you to think, reflect, and apply this material, to *practice* the principles contained herein.

Meet the Players

Do you want to be an amateur, a semipro, or a professional in your career? I use this sports analogy not only because I think everyone understands how people progress in sports, but also because applying the material in this book, like developing athletic skill, takes practice. In Chapters 5 through 12, I use three characters to illustrate these different levels of handling challenges presented in this book.

Tony, the amateur, is extraverted, aggressive, and spontaneous. He is very self-confident and likes to argue. Not everyone thinks his self-confidence is totally deserved. Tony starts his journey in Chapter 5 as a freshman at a large state college. He is undecided about a major and has a 2.0 GPA (grade point average) after one semester, but he thinks he wants to go to law school.

Tony's family business is a law firm. His dad works as the office manager, and his mom is the partner in charge of the other four lawyers in the firm. It is a first-generation family business, so Tony would be the second generation if he joins. In his family, Tony is the oldest of three boys. He feels that because his folks started and own the firm that they can do whatever they want with it. They have told him that he can work there as a lawyer if he wants. He has gone into the office a few times, and once *told* one of his mom's assistants to type one of his papers for school.

 Selina, the semipro, is introverted, thoughtful, and slow to make a decision. She is a little bit shy and likes to think things through. Her self-confidence is not her strong suit at this stage of her life. In fact, most people see her as even more credible than she sees herself. Selina also starts her journey as a freshman at a middle-sized private college. She is majoring in accounting and has a 3.0 GPA after one semester.

Selina's parents own a franchise of three restaurants. Her mom and dad were both born outside the United States and pretty much run the restaurants together; they both have college degrees, though not in business. In Selina's family, she is the middle child with an older sister and a younger brother. Her older sister just started working in the family business two years ago.

 Pat is slightly extraverted, likes to plan, and can sometimes rush to make a decision. Her self-confidence has really started to grow over the last semester at college. Pat is a freshman at a small private college with a family business program. She is interested in pursuing both finance and family business majors, and she has a 3.6 GPA. Her self-confidence is higher than most of her peers, and most people would tell you that Pat has earned it.

Pat's parents own a chain of hotels that operate in three states. Her grandmother started the chain in 1965. Pat's mother has a degree in hospitality, and her dad has a business degree. In the family, Pat is the younger of two sisters.

Use This Book as a Guide

Based on one of the most experienced programs in the world for helping the next generation in family business, this book can act as a guide or road map to help you manage the opportunity that having a family who own and operate a business presents. Eight challenges lie ahead: Within each there is great opportunity and also great risk.

During my 17 years in the academic world, I have observed two dynamics that motivated me to write this book. First, three years after graduation 80 percent of graduates will have changed career paths at least once. Secondly, of the people who quickly change career paths after college, more than 80 percent do so because they don't meet the eight challenges outlined in this book. I personally believe this condition is unacceptable in a competitive society.

My proactive response is the book you are about to read, enjoy, and, I hope, put to good use. This book doesn't just tell you that you need to plan; it shows you how to plan. It starts you on a career path through the development and use of the McCann Action Plan for Life, which will improve the likelihood of identifying a career plan that aligns with who you are and the skills you have and thereby improve the odds that you will find success and happiness in your career.

Think of it as your personal trainer for helping you develop your credibility and marketability. The book can help you, but in order to get in shape, you have to do the sweating. As I say to my students, I *believe in you and I expect more from you.* Congratulations on taking the first step toward your personal success.

PART I

Understanding Your Family Business Issues

P art I lays the groundwork for you to address the challenges that you face (or avoid) as you consider a career in your family's business or elsewhere. These introductory chapters explore a way of looking at family business and even your life as a whole in a way that you might not have ever considered. For example, Chapter 1 describes how growing up in a family that owns a business is different than growing up with parents who work for somebody else.

Chapter 2 talks about the foundation for everything that follows, having the right attitude. The right attitude is as necessary for your success as canvas is for a painting. What is the right attitude? It's being responsible for your life and taking ownership of your own success and happiness.

Chapter 3 explains systems thinking and how to look at areas of your life more holistically. It may sound complicated, but once you understand this perspective, you will never look at your family business or even your life in the same way. Few people have this kind of insight into these issues.

In Chapter 4, you confront the biggest hurdle to your success, the force that makes all eight of the challenges so difficult: emotional resistance. This may the most important single chapter in the book. If you can begin to work with your emotional resistance, you are halfway to success.

CHAPTER I

Growing Up with a Family Business

T his chapter explores what it means to grow up in a family business, how that opportunity affects your life, and what challenges it presents. Combining family and business makes life more complex because the upsides and downsides of your actions are greater than if your personal and professional lives were completely separate. Therefore, you need to take ownership of your future, not let someone else write your script for you. You also need to earn credibility and marketability. No one can give you these attributes. Without them, you will probably be unhappy and unable to contribute to your family business or any other career.

By the end of this chapter you will be able to understand

- How growing up in a family that owns a business is different from growing up in other types of families.

- What potential risks and rewards arise from being the next generation in a family business.

- Why earning credibility and marketability is crucial to your happiness.

Being a Part of the Next Generation

Growing up in a family that owns a business differs from growing up with parents that have other kinds of jobs in several ways. Growing up in a business-owning family is a little bit like being the preacher's kid in that everyone will relate what you do back to your family and its business. Because the family name is connected to the business, your parents may be even more sensitive to people saying things like, "There goes that McCann kid, always thinking he is better than everyone else and always getting into trouble." (Of course, I never did anything that would provoke such comments when I was a kid.) In a family business, the business often defines the family's identity.

Because of the family business, you may have been more involved with your parents' careers during your childhood than most kids. For example, your friends might never have even visited their parents' workplaces, but you may have had to work in your family's business. Many families with businesses need their children's help and feel that this type of experience is a great way to instill a good work ethic. Consequently, you may have had the chance to learn more responsibility at an early age than many of your peers. This experience also may have made you feel more connected with your parents. At the same time, you may have had less contact with people and situations outside of the family. You may have received less feedback than if you had worked for a nonrelative, so your work experiences may have given you less basis for comparison with other jobs.

Every family has rules, but the rules are different in a family that owns a business in that they often relate to the family's wealth. For example, many families have this rule: Never tell people about the family finances. Money is a touchy subject for most families, but when the family owns a business, it becomes even more sensitive. When I first meet with family business clients and am still establishing trust, they may be just as private with financial issues as they are with family matters. Even in my course work, parents are often most concerned about disclosing financial information. (By the way, my students never have to disclose any financial information as part of the family business program, and all the students sign confidentiality agreements.)

All families have conflicts, and most have conflicts they don't confront directly. Families tend to prefer harmony. Some families go so far as to have an implicit rule barring talk about a family conflict. When a family owns a business, there are many more opportunities for conflicts to arise because family members' careers and wealth are so connected. Perhaps you don't speak to your cousins because their dad and your dad fought over the business a long time ago, and your dad bought out your uncle. Maybe you have always sensed that there is some tension between your dad and his sister, but no one ever explains why. The reason could be that your grandfather gave your aunt a big chunk of money and your dad a big chunk of stock. Grandpa never discussed this decision with either of them, and now, years later, one of them is resentful. Maybe your aunt resents your father because the stock is worth a lot more, and she spent the money years ago. Or maybe your dad feels resentful because the business was failing, and he would have preferred the cold hard cash to the burden of owning a failing company. You grow up knowing that these topics are not cocktail party conversation.

As you have grown up with your family business, you may have made assumptions concerning the business. The most common assumption is that everyone in the family is entitled to a job in the family business. Usually families don't talk about these assumptions, yet family members still act as though they are true. In my experience, however, accepting these assumptions as fact is a big mistake. One of my students was certain his father wanted him to join the family business at graduation. When he interviewed his father for a class project, however, he found out his father planned on selling the business within the next year and retiring. He learned a hard lesson about making assumptions.

Up until this point, you might not have thought much about the way your family handles things or considered that other families or businesses do things differently. I hope that with this book you will become more aware of issues within the family business so that you can make informed choices about your life and career. As you go through the book, you'll have chances to step back and take a fresh look at things you may have been taking for granted. (If you are a parent, you may want to download the free parents' guide to using this book from www.gregmccannspeaks.com).

Managing Transitions Through Life's Stages

Every living thing from trees to cows and even organizations goes through *life* stages. "To everything there is a season," as the Bible and the rock group the Byrds say (Ecclesiastes 3:1 and the song "Turn, Turn, Turn"). Recognizing that your life, your family, and your family's business go through stages can help you in a couple of ways.

> **KEYWORD:** Life stages are the phases that individuals, families and even family businesses go through. They may not happen exactly at the same time for everyone, but they are the typical, normal transitions that everyone goes through.

First, knowing about life stages helps you see what lies ahead. If you had to drive from your house to my house, wouldn't it help to have a roadmap and maybe some hints about how to avoid the obstacles? A roadmap lets you learn from others who have already traveled ahead. You gain from their experience. Even though the journey will be your own, you don't have to do it without help. This book can be a roadmap for your transitions. If you can see the predictable transitions for you, your family, and your family business, then you can prepare for them. You know they are coming; the only decision is how you want to deal with them. Put another way, once you become aware of what lies ahead, you can start making better choices.

The second benefit to learning about life stages is that doing so can help you *normalize* your transitions. For example, individuation, which I talk about in Chapter 2, is a transition that is a typical part of every young person's life. In my work as a family business consultant, I see many families that are having trouble with a transition. Often, the trouble arises because they haven't undergone this kind of transition before.

KEYWORD: To **normalize** is to go through the process of recognizing that the difficulties you face during life stage transitions are typical. Practically all families that have businesses go through transitions similar to the ones your family has faced in the past, faces in the present, or will face in the future. In a sense, you feel more "normal" because you understand that practically everyone goes through what you are going through.

Adult Life Stages

In the book *Working with Family Businesses* (Jossey-Bass, 1996), author David Bork identifies the major life stages that individuals, families, and family businesses go through. Table 1.1 lists the adult life stages for an individual.

Table 1.1 Adult Life Stages

Age	Life Stage
17-22	Transition to early adulthood
22-28	Entry into adult world
28-33	Age 30 transition
33-40	Settling-down phase
40-45	Midlife transition
45-50	Beginning mid-adulthood
50-55	Age 50 transition
55-60	Ending of mid-adulthood
60-65	Late adulthood transition
60+	Late adulthood

Between the ages of 17 and 25, you experience one or maybe two life transitions. First, you transition from a child into a young adult. During this transition, you test boundaries; establish your own values, beliefs, and attitudes; and often defy your parents. You are likely to distance yourself from your parents and then, in the next transition, to experience a need to reconnect with them as adults.

From about 22 to 28, many people start to establish themselves in the adult world, which means their focus shifts to family and career. As David Bork points out, navigating these changes while working with your family or even just dealing with the influence of their wealth creates more challenges than other people typically have to face.

Family Life Stages

Just as you move through individual life stages, families also go through life stages, from being newlyweds to having small children, to having teenagers, to living in an empty nest, and finally to retiring. Newborn children, like newborn businesses, take a lot of time and can demand attention at all hours. Dealing with teenagers is a humbling experience. They pull away, convinced their parents are among the dumbest, most uncool people on the planet, and suddenly they like everything their parents hate. Having a family business means the changes wrought during these family life stages are more connected on individual and business levels as well.

Family Business Life Stages

Just like individuals and families, family businesses also go through major life stages:

> Start-up
> Growth
> Renewal

The start-up stage is tough. It only happens once, and this stage is when most family businesses fail, which in part is why it is so demanding. During the growth stage, the business changes from a one-person autocratic entity to an organization where the power is shared. Especially in a family business, this transition means redefining how to distribute the power of the family, the management of the business, and the ownership and governance of the business.

You may have sensed that the transition from the first generation to the second is often the hardest one for a family business. This transition frequently involves shifting away from one parent controlling the family, the management of the business, and both the family's wealth and family business ownership. These changes are difficult, and they sometimes occur simultaneously.

But growth in the second generation and beyond is not easy, either. Nor is it easy to renew a family business. All of these transitions mean that each generation has to decide why it has this business and why this business has this generation of the family involved.

Facing the Family Business Challenge

No family is simple. When you add a business to a family, the situation becomes even more complex. In short, the good stuff can be better, and the bad stuff can be even worse. The following sections describe the characteristics of this work/life combination that make it unique.

The Connection Between the Family and the Business

Especially in the first generation, the generation that starts the business, the family's ownership and operation of the business tightly connects the family to the business. As a result, changes in the family or the business affect each other far more than a change would if the family did not have a business. For example, a divorce in a first-generation family business causes profound changes for the family and the business. If that same couple worked at IBM and Dell, for example, the divorce would have much less impact on their workplaces. As you can see, combining family and business can have some amazing benefits, but it is not without its complexities and challenges.

Starting and running a family business demands a lot of attention. This situation can unite the family members around a shared passion and common challenges. If everyone at the dinner table is committed to the success of the family business, that commitment can add meaning to the lives of individual family members while strengthening the bonds between them. For example, I started working in my dad's business at age 11, which gave me a chance to begin to understand how he spent his days. Especially when the children are young, many parents use that sense of commitment to the family business to instill a strong work ethic in their kids.

However, the potential downside to a family business is that parents who are focused on the family business may pay less attention to the other areas of their children's lives. They may be more likely to miss school plays and soccer games. They may also be less able to get away from work for a few hours to help with homework or for a few days to take the family on a vacation. Sometimes it may seem as though the business always comes first. That situation can create anger and resentment. Children may feel neglected and may decide to behave badly in order to get attention from their parents.

This deep connection between the family and the business coupled with a lack of experience managing the family involvement and the family/business boundaries makes for a difficult situation for the first-generation family business in particular. However, all generations have to deal with these kinds of issues. When the boundaries between family and business blur, dinnertime becomes a place to talk about the business. The office becomes a place where the argument about a mother-in-law continues from the dinner table to the conference room.

Realize that the greater the involvement of the family in the business, the greater the impact changes in the family will have on the business and vice versa. Chapter 3 delves deeper into this topic with its discussion of systems, but for now take a moment to consider how connected your family is to the business:

1. How many people work in the business? How many of those are family members? Having a significant percentage of people in the business who are family members, especially at the managerial level, indicates a strong family connection to the business.

2. How many people have a financial or emotional sense of ownership of the business? The more people that feel ownership (emotionally, not necessarily legally) the greater the connection is, and the more everything affects everything else.

3. Is the family name part of the business name?

4. Has the business been in the family for several generations?

5. Do your parents have their life savings invested in it?

If you answered yes to questions 3, 4, and 5, then your family is most likely very connected with the business.

To get a sense of how connected your parents may feel to the business, consider a statistic mentioned in Dennis Jaffe's book Working with the Ones You Love (Conari Press, 1990). The average CEO of a large publicly traded company stays at the company less than 6 years, but the average CEO of a family business is in charge for 24 years! For the CEOs of family businesses, their positions aren't just jobs—they are their lives, their identities, and their missions. The family business is often where they put all their money, all their time, and much of their passion.

Leadership

Especially in the early stages, families and businesses are similar entities. They are usually headed by one or maybe two people who can do pretty much anything they want.

In a typical first-generation family business, one parent may take charge in the business while the other takes charge of the family. There are various combinations, but usually when the kids are young and the business is young, the power is not shared. Your parents may have said to you, as mine occasionally did, "This is not a democracy." Both the family and the business usually start out as autocratic. By autocratic, I mean one person makes the decisions. The power is not shared, and others are expected to obey and follow orders.

Perhaps the parents in a family business are no more autocratic than parents in other families. The difference is that family business parents control both the family and the business. As a result, if you are in the next generation, both your personal and professional life will be more controlled by your parents. Such control can last well into adulthood.

In an autocratic environment, the head person's personality dominates and defines the business and the family. This idea is important to understand, because it is what makes a family that owns and operates a business different from one that doesn't. If the leaders, your parents, are spontaneous, they risk imposing chaos. If they are innovative, they risk overwhelming people. The leader's personality shapes the personality and values of the business and the family.

Lack of Feedback

Another trait of autocracies is that the one or two people in charge are less likely to get feedback. This lack of feedback means that the family and the business are less able and less likely to be self-correcting. Because they aren't getting the information about what is wrong, they are more likely to continue behavior that isn't healthy. It is a little like never having anyone who will tell you when you have food stuck in your teeth. It is hard to fix something if no one tells you it needs fixing.

Again, this lack of feedback is most often true in the early stages of the family and the business. In the family setting, young children may not have the awareness or assertiveness to confront their parents. Many corporations have boards of directors or advisors who both monitor the actions and decisions of management and give the management feedback. But in a family business where the parents are both the owners and the managers, this type of oversight typically does not exist. Chapter 12 explains the challenges of this issue in greater detail.

Competing Goals

To understand family business, you need to understand how businesses and families are different. Table 1.2 outlines the main differences between these two types of organizations.

Table 1.2 How Family and Business Compare

Family	Business
Permanent relationships	More temporary relationships
Unconditional love	Conditional approval
Roles based on relationships	Roles based on functions
Goal is to maintain harmony	Goal is to maintain productivity
Power based on generational status	Power based on performance and title
Fairness means the same/equal	Fairness based on performance/equity

Think about how the titles and names of family roles and business roles differ. In a family, people usually are called by a name that defines their relationship, such as Mom, Uncle, or Grandpa. People in business are usually referred to by a title that tells you what they do, such as Manager, Director of Sales, CEO. This comparison illustrates the biggest difference between a family and a business. Families focus on relationships, and businesses focus more on actions and results.

Families tend to focus on things such as harmony, relationships, connection, and the well-being of the individuals within the family. In a family, treating people fairly usually means treating them the same. That's especially true when it comes to the parents' treatment of the next generation. Businesses, on the other hand, tend to focus on things such as growth, performance, competence, and profit. Treating people fairly in a business means treating them based on how well they perform.

Family relationships are permanent and based on unconditional love. You never have had a performance review as a sibling, have you? However, businesses are based on temporary and conditional relationships that focus on performance. Your boss is not likely to say to you, "I know you failed miserably on your sales goals, but I still love you as my sales manager. Come on and give me a hug." If he did, that would certainly be a strange day at work.

Of course, the family organization and the business organization often overlap in a family business. For example, a mother might have to decide whether to hire her daughter. This overlap creates a struggle between family goals and business goals. Well-meaning parents sometimes make business decisions based on family criteria instead of business criteria. I had one client, a parent, who felt her eldest son who worked in the family business deserved a raise because his younger sister, who worked in another business in another industry in a different city, had gotten a raise. Can you see how the family rules of harmony and fairness are different than the business rules of competence and merit?

When a family manages its involvement in the family business well, people have more trust in the business, and the business management can make plans for the long term. Family members can then use their shared passion to create a legacy and ensure the economic security. When family goals and business goals are acknowledged to be separate but related, family members, especially the next generation, are better able to develop their potential.

Wealth and Power

I discuss wealth and power in more detail in Chapter 6, but I want to address it briefly here. Wealth is a challenging subject. Just having wealth, be it sudden or earned, does not guarantee happiness.

Wealth is a challenge to a family for two main reasons. First, it is often the bargaining chip for emotions. The person who controls the wealth often uses it or is perceived as using it to make sure they get what they want emotionally. For example, no one wants to make old Aunt Erma angry if she is 90, controls all the wealth and ownership in the family business, and tells you that she has her will written in pencil so she can change it easily. Under those conditions, you would be pretty happy to join her 23 cats for dinner at her house, wouldn't you?

Wealth is a two-sided coin for everyone, but it is especially challenging for young adults who are trying to figure out who they want to be. I believe, as do many others, that there is no personal growth without personal struggle. When wealth takes away the necessary struggle, and thus the growth that would have resulted from it, then wealth is corrupting.

Test Your Mettle

Steven Rockefeller, Jr., a fifth-generation member of one of the most successful and wealthiest families in history, once came to Stetson University to speak to the students. Steven talked about how he left home to spend time working on a boat, fishing for king crabs in Alaska. Working on a fishing boat, especially crabbing in the cold Arctic waters, is a dangerous, difficult, and unglamorous job. However, Steven believed money did not grant him an easy life, but one of greater opportunity. His maternal grandfather had fished the North Sea, and the young Rockefeller felt called to do likewise. Testing his mettle, he believed, was a necessary part of his personal growth.

The Core Question for Any Family in Business

I always ask my clients this serious question: Why does this family have this business, and why does this business have this family? Most clients answer that their family has this business because of some connection the founder had to it. That is a start, but it does not truly answer why the current generation still owns the business.

None of my clients have, at least initially, been able to clearly and collectively state how the business benefits from having *this family* involved. That is a great place to begin some deep thinking about making sure the family business benefits the family and benefits the business. Taking ownership for the connection between family and business means you should make sure the family and the business benefit from one another's involvement. To not do so is to put both at risk.

Managing Opportunities and Relationships

If your family has a business, you have greater opportunities, but also greater risks. The challenge is to manage your actions so that you avoid the risk and take advantage of the opportunity.

Many next-generation people think of the family business as a one-time career choice. The moment you graduate, you have to decide: Do I take the job with my family business or not? This is a very narrow and potentially destructive perspective.

Growing up in a family that owns a business involves managing three potentially lifelong roles and sets of responsibilities. As a member of the next generation, you have the role of (potential) employee, of (potential) owner or heir, and of a more closely connected family member. In the article "The Influence of Life Stages on Father-Son Work Relationships (*Family Business Review*, Volume 2(1), Spring 1989)," authors John A. Davis and Renato Tagiuri portrayed these roles as three overlapping circles (see Figure 1.1). The following sections discuss how you can manage these roles.

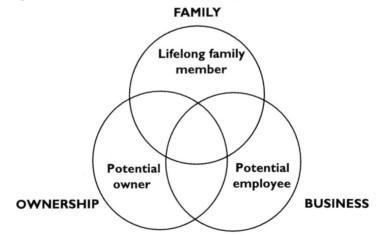

Figure 1.1 Davis and Tagiuri's three-circle model for the roles in a family business.

How Do You Handle Your Family Business Roles?

First, consider your role as a family member. You will probably be more connected with your family than most people. Richard Narva, a colleague and noted family business consultant, points out that it is fairly easy to navigate your crazy relatives for a day or two over the holidays, but it is much more difficult to work with them 50 to 80 hours a week and link your future to them.

Second, consider your role as a potential employee, which could mean assuming a leadership position in your family business. Ask yourself these questions:

- When, how, and why should you join the family business?
- Should you join the family business at all?
- Should you have outside experience before joining the family business?
- Can you agree on an exit strategy that allows you to preserve your family relationships in case you want to leave or the family business wants you to leave?

The third role, and the one that may seem the farthest off, is that of potential heir to the family wealth and potential owner of the family business. Consider the following questions:

- What does your family's wealth mean to you?
- What expectations do your parents have related to the wealth?
- When do you get a share of the wealth?
- Do you have control over it, or are there conditions?

What about owning a part of the family business? Ownership can mean you have the right to receive distributions (that is, cash) and govern the company. So can you just kick back and receive distributions as though the family business is your personal ATM machine or are there responsibilities that come with ownership? What are these responsibilities? How much control do you have over the family business?

The owners of the company are supposed to govern it. That means they set the long-term vision, they hold management accountable, and they may even have to put more of their own personal money into the company. Nothing can destroy the sustainability of a family business like owners who don't take ownership.

Which Hat Are You Wearing?

In the book *Working with Family Businesses* (Jossey-Bass, 1996), author David Bork asks readers to imagine three hats. One is labeled *family*, one is labeled *employee*, and the third is labeled *owner/heir*. Watch as you go through your week to see whether you are wearing different hats or even more than one hat at a time. Notice which hats your parents are wearing, too.

Suppose your mom is the president of the family business and your dad is a vice president. Your dad says that he wants a raise from your mom, his boss. He says he has earned it because he does all the work around the house. Can you see how he is mixing family and business roles? He is arguing that because he does certain things, like the housework, in his role as the family member he deserves to be compensated in his business role of vice president. Mixing these roles is like wearing two hats at the same time—it just doesn't work. Keep this idea in mind. I will come back to it in Chapter 3.

Developing Credibility and Marketability

Any young person entering adulthood needs to develop two traits, which are also the two core benefits of Stetson University's undergraduate program in family business. The first is *credibility*, which I define as legitimate self-confidence. If you think you are God's gift to the world but no one shares your opinion, then you do not have credibility.

The second trait, *marketability*, is the other side of that coin. Does the marketplace value the skills, credentials, and experiences you have developed? If you want to work in the business world (or get hired by anyone besides your family), then you need marketability.

> **KEYWORD:** Credibility is when you feel self-confident and other people can legitimately validate that feeling. It has both an internal and an external aspect, and you need both. **Marketability** is having the skills, credentials, and experiences needed to succeed in a career that you want to pursue.

Every young person faces the challenge of developing these two traits. But if your family owns a business, that challenge can be harder for you. Why would that be, you wonder? Because you don't have the positive pressure to understand that you need to develop these two traits. You can be seduced into thinking that you don't have to develop credibility and marketability, and therefore can waste your college years. Likewise, you can be misled into thinking you already have them, as when some well-intentioned but misguided parent says, "Son, at 16 you already know more than my three top guys who are all in their 50s," even when no one else has that perception.

I discuss tools for developing credibility in Chapter 13 and for developing marketability in Chapter 14. Before that, I explain the eight challenges you will face in developing these traits and how to deal with them.

Conclusion

As you have learned in this chapter, business and family are connected to one another through the family business, and the points where they overlap create great risks and opportunity. Your biggest challenge is to maximize the opportunity of growing up with a family business while minimizing the risks.

Keep the following ideas from this chapter in mind as you work your way through the rest of this book:

• The predictable transitions in your life, your family's life, and your family's business will all affect one another.

Continued

Continued

- Growing up with a family business means that you have to deal with issues concerning family roles, work/life balance, career planning, and wealth in a way that most people don't.
- You can be handed many things on a silver platter, but credibility and marketability, like happiness, must be earned. Having an attitude of entitlement will threaten both your credibility and marketability and ultimately your happiness.

CHAPTER 2

Taking Ownership of Your Life

Are you ready, willing, and able to take ownership for your life from this moment on? If you want to be your own person, then you must face the challenges that come with making your own decisions and living with the consequences.

The concept of personal ownership for your life is a theme throughout this book. Taking ownership for your life is as important to your success and credibility as sitting in the driver's seat is to driving a car. It may not always take you where you want to go, but it is a very important place from which to start.

By the end of this chapter, you will be able to understand the importance of
- Establishing an emotional self that is separate from your family.
- Examining your behavior patterns.
- Focusing on how you handle the three major roles in your life.

Becoming an Individual

Between the ages of 15 and 25, you go through a life-changing transition from childhood to adulthood called *individuation*. The concept of individuation comes from the psychological study of families and family systems. During this transition, you develop an identity that is distinct and separate from your parents. In short, you start to become an adult.

KEYWORD: Individuation is the process whereby you evolve into your own person with your own feelings, ideas, beliefs, and values.

When you were living at home and going to high school, your parents looked out for you, and maybe your teachers and coaches did, too. If you missed the bus, did you blame it on your parents? Did your teachers remind you about assignments or give you extra credit to help you make up for not studying? Did your coaches follow up with your teachers and your parents to make sure you were doing well in school and at home? These actions are appropriate when you are a child, when you have not yet fully become your own person. But as you head off to college or otherwise start out on your own, thinking that someone else is responsible for your life can become a big problem.

Some people avoid the process of individuation for years or even their entire lives. Separating from your family is difficult, particularly if you are part of a business-owning family, but you have to be individuated before you can take ownership for your life.

Having Your Own Emotions

You may or may not adopt the same viewpoint or feelings that your parents have, but individuation means your emotions are truly your own. Just because your parents feel one way or have a belief about something does not mean you have to feel or believe the same thing. Of course, your family, and especially your parents, will affect the way you feel to some degree.

You can view the process of emotional individuation as a continuum from enmeshed to detached. Someone who is enmeshed is very emotionally connected, perhaps too connected, to his or her family. For example, when Dad walks in from work upset about not getting a loan from the bank, the enmeshed family members in the house instantly become angry, too—even before Dad tells them why he's upset. At the other extreme, a detached person has little or no emotional connection to the family. I always think of detached people as being like the Vulcans on *Star Trek*. If Dad says he didn't get the loan and he has to declare bankruptcy, a detached person might just say, "That ought to be interesting. I have always wanted to learn more about how bankruptcy works."

Emotionally healthy family members are somewhere in the middle. They may feel for Dad, and they may get a little upset after hearing what happened to him, but they have their own emotional responses. The family members are close, connected, and concerned, but they still have separate identities, emotions, and opinions. This separation is, or should be, a big difference between a 2-year-old and a 25-year-old. The 2-year-old will cry when he sees his parents cry, without knowing why. An individuated 25-year-old will be concerned, but he won't merely react.

Defining Your Own Boundaries

If you're between 15 and 25, your current stage of life is about exploring your personality, testing limits, and experimenting. Within reason, all those activities can be healthy, so go ahead and hear someone lecture on anarchy, read a book on alternative lifestyles, or learn about the art that your mom has always hated.

Testing the boundaries can be fine, but there's a risk that you can get stuck in the testing stage instead of truly establishing who you are. Taking one of the two extreme approaches to testing boundaries, *compliance and defiance*, will keep you from taking ownership for your life.

Compliance means doing what someone else wants you to do. In the context of families, it often means doing everything your parents want you to do. It is the way a good little boy or girl is supposed to act. Being compliant discounts your needs, stops you from finding out who you are, and undermines what you and your parents really want, which is for you to create your own happiness.

Defiance, on the other hand, means not doing what your parents want. Although the behavior is the opposite of compliance, it has the same result: It keeps you from figuring out who you really are. If your dad tells you not to date crazy bikers, but you do it just to defy him, not because you really like crazy bikers, then you are no closer to being authentic than someone who is stuck in compliance. (By the way, police sirens and high-speed chases get old fast.)

KEYWORD: Compliance is a pattern of doing what your parents or family members want without considering what you really want. Defiance is a pattern of not doing what your parents or family members want instead of considering what you really want.

Chances are, you'll more likely be compliant rather than defiant in a family that has a family business. Why? Because such families tend to be closer, and defiance is a little tougher to pull off when your folks are your bosses as well as your parents. However, it isn't the fact that your behavior complies or defies that is important, it is the fact that you are following a pattern of always agreeing or always disagreeing with your family. Virtually no one sees this point very clearly at first. We all tend to lean towards one end of the continuum, but your goal should be to break out of your pattern and achieve authenticity by deciding for yourself what to do (see Figure 2.1).

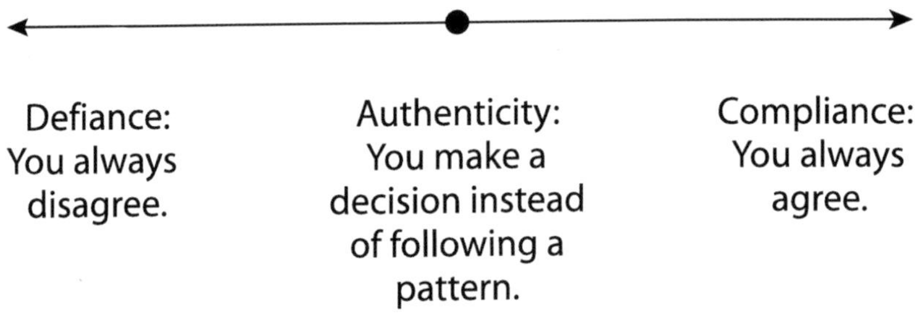

| Defiance: You always disagree. | Authenticity: You make a decision instead of following a pattern. | Compliance: You always agree. |

Figure 2.1 The defiance/compliance scale.

I once worked with a colleague to consult with a family business that included five members of the next generation, ranging in age from 30s to early 50s. Two were pretty darned compliant, and two were very defiant. Only one was fairly clear about what she wanted. Interestingly, she was the only one who did not live in the same town and did not work in the business, although she was involved in the ownership of the business and had worked in the business in the past. The other four siblings had to take a hard look at the behavior patterns in which they were stuck, automatically accepting or rejecting their parents' every suggestion. Don't fall into that trap—it serves no one.

Making the Transition

Taking ownership for your life is hard work. It involves taking the time to reflect on and address important personal issues. An important part of this work is setting goals and planning for your future. This work is so important that the students in the family business program at Stetson University are required to write a 30- to 50-page paper that follows the McCann Action Plan (MAP) for Life outline to help them deal with these issues. (The MAP for Life is discussed in detail in Chapter 13.) Is all the hard work worth it? Most students in my family business course think so. They consistently rate the course a 10 out of 10 on practical value.

This process of taking ownership is like getting in shape. If you don't lift the weights and sweat, you won't get into shape. But if you do the necessary work, you will end up in that elite group of people your age who figure out who they are, live and work in accordance with their values, and make the family business a healthy opportunity. But like getting into shape, there are pitfalls that can keep you from making progress. Falling into emotional patterns and being a victim can keep you from taking full ownership of your life.

Watch for Patterns

Look for emotional *patterns* in your life, those repeated choices that you are no longer making consciously. For example, if you automatically get angry every time your dad gives you advice, then you are caught up in a pattern.

> **KEYWORD:** **Patterns** are repetitive, reactive behaviors. People often repeat patterns without being consciously aware of the choice they are making.

Consider what other choices you have. Once you begin to see that a pattern contains the potential for you to rethink your choices, you will no longer feel stuck. You can begin to make changes in your attitude, your behavior, and your emotions, even if the other person never changes. Often, if you start to work on yourself, then you'll reap an amazing benefit. You will create a role model of someone working on themselves as well as the opportunity for the other person to change, too.

Progress is the result of your working to improve. Like an athlete, you put in the time, you keep at it, you set goals, you measure your performance, and you may even engage a coach or friend to help you continue to improve.

Don't Be a Victim

There are people who suffer from true tragedies, such as illnesses, accidents, or crime, and then there are those who simply don't take ownership for their roles in their daily lives and relationships. As my father says, if you are hit by lightning, you deserve sympathy. If you drive your car with the oil warning light on for 500 miles and your engine blows up, you deserve far less sympathy. If something is foreseeable and predictable, you have a choice; you are not a victim.

Look at the problems you have with your relationships, and consider whether you are playing the role of a victim. If so, is the problem more like the lightning where there is nothing you can do, or is it more like the engine warning light that has been on for a long time? There are predictable and foreseeable changes we all have to face while growing up and becoming ourselves. Once you become aware, you know the warning light is on, and you have a choice about how to react.

In my family business course, I talk about why you shouldn't think of yourself as a victim. Victims are people who have no control or choice about what happens to them or how they respond. The upside to being a victim is that you don't have to take responsibility for anything: "The lightning just came out of nowhere." You can then take up the victim's favorite hobby-complaining. You can sit around with friends and cry in your beer, saying, "Aren't the problems in my life just wrong? Isn't it sad what's happened to me?"

The downside of being a victim is that nothing ever changes, and it feels as if there is no way out. But if you become aware of your tendency toward self-victimization, you can use that awareness to understand yourself and grow. I believe that if you become more self-aware, you can make better choices.

Suppose that every time your mother criticizes you, you get angry, blow up, withdraw for a day or so, and then feel lousy. How do you keep this from happening? If mom does X (criticizes you) and you automatically respond with Y (getting angry and beating yourself up), then you're stuck. That leads to one of my favorite questions: What do you need to do if the other person never changes?

People often say, "If only she would change, then I would be happy." Think about the significance of that statement. If you give that much power to another person, then you give up your own power to be happy. In effect, you are saying, "I am a victim. There is nothing I can do." Don't fall into this sense of helplessness! At best, it gets you other people's sympathy. At worst, it condemns you to a life of suffering.

Do you blame your parents for your problems? Are you waiting for other people to change so that you can be happy? If so, then you have a victim's attitude. To stop thinking like a victim, you first need to realize that your reaction to your mom's criticism is more your problem than hers. Your ability to choose your response is the difference between being a victim and not being one.

You are at a crossroads in your life. Are you ready to commit to not being a victim? When I teach the family business class I mentioned, about 10 percent of the students drop out. Why? Some could argue that my sense of humor is the reason, but I would bet it is because they aren't ready.

One semester, a student said in the middle of the discussion about being a victim, "Being accountable is hard." He was right—growing up is hard. I won't tell you it's not, but I will say that not being accountable and not growing up is a certain path to misery for you and your family.

In college, I hear many students talk about graduation as a cliff. They talk about going into the family business or graduate school merely to avoid taking ownership for their lives. Individuation is a transition that needs to be faced, whether at age 15 or 50. It does not get any easier as you get older, in part because when you have a full-time job, a spouse, kids, and bills to pay, time for reflection is far harder to find. I had one client in his 50s who told me he had sold his soul to his family business, and now, at this relatively late stage, he was finally beginning to find his own life. Ask yourself how ready you are to take ownership for your future.

Addressing the Three Roles in Your Life

Essentially, this book is meant to help you take ownership for your life. This task may be very difficult to do, at least at first. An important factor in taking ownership is managing the three lifelong roles described in Chapter 1: family member, potential employee/leader in the family business, and potential owner or heir to the family wealth. How do you address these three roles in your life?

Your Role as a Family Member

As any leadership book will tell you, success starts with a self-assessment. That is, success begins with taking a hard look at yourself. This assessment relates to your role as a family member, but clarifying who you are will also help you in the other two roles, employee and owner, should you choose to accept them.

Teenagers start off avoiding self-reflection, learning about themselves, or taking ownership for their behavior. For teenagers who are part of a business-owning family, the family business often can be a tempting haven because they think, "I can do anything I like because my parents own the business. I can avoid accountability. I can avoid addressing some of my bad habits, like being late. I can look to my parents to make me happy." As you might imagine, there is often a gap between how the people at this stage see themselves and how others see them.

Most people eventually begin to ask themselves self-assessment questions: Who am I? What do I want to do with my life? What are my core values? But many find it hard to maintain their attention and to commit to self-reflection, feedback, and self-development on an ongoing basis. Some people never evolve beyond this stage. There are others who want to be better, but can't quite figure out how to do it, where to go for help, and what tools to use. They often feel stuck, frustrated, and confused.

I'm going to digress a minute and tell you something about my reason for writing this book. After years of work on myself (which, like trying to stay in shape, is an ongoing part of life), I realize that the value at the core of my teaching and consulting is the desire to work with people who want to work. I wrote this book for people who want to work, too. Are you willing to work? Are you willing to grow from where you are right now toward being more professional and more responsible for your life? Bottom line: Are you ready to take ownership for your life and your future?

Socrates said, "The unexamined life is not worth living." Are you willing to admit that you need to work on being aware? To become self-aware, you need to ask others for feedback. Through this feedback, you will develop a self-perception that is pretty similar to how others see you. At this level of maturity and development, you should be willing to sacrifice short-term comfort (because some of the feedback you hear might be constructive criticism) for long-term gain (as you develop a practice to align your behavior with both who you are and where you want to go). Maintaining your life at this level is an ongoing practice.

Your Role as an Employee

It's easy to be seduced and corrupted by the opportunity represented by a family business. Having that opportunity readily available might mean you don't have to take ownership for your decision about what to do with your life because that decision is already made. On that level, you might think you don't have to work and earn a legitimate sense of self-confidence or what this book calls credibility. But if you stay at that level, you never develop the skills, credentials, and experiences necessary to *earn* a job, and you never learn that you have to be marketable.

As you grow and mature, you will want to decide what to do with your career, and you may be unsure what to do with your opportunity to enter the family business. Perhaps you can't quite figure out if working in the family business is best, or if it is just being compliant. Perhaps it is wiser to work outside the family business or is that just being defiant? It is hard to know what is the best thing to do.

Even if you know what's best for you, doing what's best can be hard. Your family and friends may have the best intentions in the world, but they could actually be working against you. I see friends of young people who very eagerly advise them to take the more immature route in their career. "Dude, take that cushy job with your folks and just chill," they'll say, but they don't know where that path leads.

The more evolved and mature person has invested the sweat and done the hard work to align her self-assessment with her career choices. She realizes that in today's world learning how to pick a career is vital. She knows that the family business is an opportunity, but it is one that must be managed and not misused. She has committed herself to cultivating her credibility and her marketability. She is aware that entering her family business for the wrong reasons can hurt not only her own credibility, but also that of her family business and even her family.

Your Role as Owner and/or Heir

An immature person will use the family's wealth and related power in ways that ultimately erode his credibility and marketability. He is willing to drive an expensive car that he did not earn and otherwise avail himself of the luxuries wealth affords, but he doesn't invest in developing himself, giving back to charitable causes, or learning about stewardship (this concept is covered in Chapter 6).

All the money in the world can't buy you credibility. When not used wisely, money and power can create distractions and rationalizations that keep you from doing the hard work necessary to earn credibility. Legitimate self-confidence comes through trying things, testing yourself, expanding your capacity, and helping others. Having money makes it easy to avoid those tasks.

A person with money and no maturity is like the athlete who never goes to the gym and just shows up on game day: He isn't prepared for the game.

People who are not ready to take ownership for their lives can also use their wealth and power to avoid taking responsibility for their behavior. We have all seen how the world allows rich and powerful people to get away with things. I had one student whose family was very wealthy, and people were constantly giving him extensions and special privileges and generally enabling him not to deal with the consequences of his behavior. When he left college, he had little credibility, and he was far from happy.

The person who is growing more mature struggles between using her money and power for efforts to develop herself and others versus indulging in wealth for entertainment and image enhancement. She is not yet clear what the wealth should mean, and she doesn't yet know what all the rules are for using it. She sees it can be used to develop herself with travel, courses, and other learning opportunities. She has even thought about working with the Peace Corps or Habitat for Humanity. But it is hard to know where to draw the line. She is concerned about what to tell her friends about the family wealth. She knows that she didn't earn it, so she is concerned about whether she deserves it.

The developed person understands that both wealth and power must be used with mindfulness. She understands what it means to be a steward of resources. That money can be used for fun—after all, she isn't an ascetic—but she realizes that things don't bring happiness. Money can be invested in her development, and it can be invested in others through charity and social causes. Money carries with it an obligation to give back to the community. Money is power and access to power. As such, it needs to be used very mindfully.

Conclusion

Becoming your own person and taking ownership for your life is an ongoing process, not a single event. This chapter presented many of the issues that you must address before you can begin to plan your life and career.

Keep these points in mind:

- Individuation is about being your own person with your own feelings and boundaries.

- Taking ownership of your life is hard work. You must examine why you make the choices you make and be accountable for those choices.

- Being able to manage the major roles in your life in a mature way is a big part of taking ownership for your life.

In the next chapter, you'll discover a new, deeper, and more insightful way to look at family business. Afterward, you will find it easier to understand the risks, identify your emotional resistance, and begin to confront it.

CHAPTER 3

Understanding Relationships in the Family and the Business

Managing your roles in your family and family business can be difficult. When you feel stuck in a difficult situation, gaining a new perspective is helpful. Where do you find this new perspective? Ask an expert! Experts in family business include people who consult to family businesses, scholars who research family business, and teachers who teach about family business. This chapter presents the experts' view on family business to help you look at your relationship with your family and your family's business in a new way.

In this chapter, you will

- Look at a family, a business, and a family business as systems.
- Analyze how you navigate your roles as a family member, as a potential employee, and as a potential owner. Knowing which role you are operating in can go a long way towards clearing up confusion and can add to your credibility.
- Learn about the transitions that you, your family, and the family business will face. This knowledge allows you to be more proactive and take greater

ownership for your life. It also enables you to really help your family business.

• Discover ways to involve your family with your efforts related to this book.

Viewing the Family Business as a System

A *system* is a group of connected parts that form an interrelated whole. You deal with systems all the time. Your body, for example, is a system made up of many smaller subsystems, such as the digestive system and the respiratory system. Likewise, the environment is a system made up of smaller ecosystems, and a computer is a system made up of smaller software systems. I want you to start to look at your family business as a system by thinking in terms of how the parts affect the whole and how the whole affects the parts.

KEYWORD: A **system** is a set of things or group of people that are interdependent and that work together as a single entity.

Consider how a world-renowned physicist might describe an object, this book in your hands, for instance, on the subatomic level. At that level, where physicists are looking at phenomena smaller than molecules, atoms, or even electrons and start talking about the quantum level, there is no mass. There's just packets of energy. How does something with no mass exist? These great minds will tell you that there is really nothing, no thing, in your hands. There are no things; there are only relationships between energy! Now if that is true of a book, then think about taking that perspective with people. To borrow the metaphor from the physicist, a group of people, a system, is nothing but relationships. If you reflect on that idea, it will blow your mind and change your perspective!

Professionals who study groups of people, including families, will tell you that the most important aspect of a group is not its individual members; the most important aspect is the relationships between those individuals. Therefore, you should think of systems, including that system called the family business, not as things or people, but as the relationships between them.

Interdependence

Picture a baby's mobile—you know, that thing that parents hang over a baby's crib that has a bunch of colorful objects hanging from strings. If you move one thing, the cow, for instance, then all the other things move. Everything is connected and interdependent, not independent. Systems work the same way.

In a system, *interdependence* means everything affects everything else. You can't shake the cow without the duck moving. You can't change the protons in this book without changing all the atoms. You can't just change one person in a family without changing the family.

> **KEYWORD:** Interdependence means that the parts affect the whole, and the whole affects the parts. The relationships between the parts or people are affected by changes in one another.

Most Americans have difficulty looking at groups of people, whether in a family or business, as systems. We think that we are independent, which is a big part of the American culture. Most of us have the perspective that, "Other people don't influence me. I decide my own behavior." Other cultures do not struggle so much with the notion of being interdependent. However, acknowledging that the groups we are a part of affect us and vice versa is an important step in solving personal and group problems.

Back in the early 1980s, one of my family's businesses ran hospitals that treated people for addictions and chemical dependency. The people in the treatment field had learned this idea of a family being a system where everyone is interdependent. Because of this perspective, they would include a patient's family for one week of the four weeks of treatment. So over a week of treatment, the family members looked at some of their patterns and made some very important choices about how to improve the situation. The patient had a far greater chance of a successful recovery if the entire family/system was involved.

When you have a systems perspective, you value decisions that are sustainable for everyone. Because you are looking out for the welfare of everyone or everything in the system, you don't want to cheat one part. For example, you don't want to disregard the older generation in a family business. You look at things more holistically, realizing how the parts affect the whole and how the whole affects the parts. This perspective goes back to one of the main themes of this book: Better awareness creates a better ability to choose the best response.

The Importance of Choice

People who study systems say the biggest difference between groups of humans and other types of systems is that humans have a choice about how to react. A forest cannot choose how to react to global warming. Its reaction is not a conscious decision; it is involuntary. Your digestive system cannot choose how to react to food poisoning. But you can choose how to react to your mom's criticism.

As the eminent mathematician Norbert Wiener said in his 1950 book *Human Use of Human Beings*, "We are not the stuff that abides, but patterns that perpetuate themselves." In human systems, behavior patterns are often choices that people are no longer consciously making. Once you become aware of the pattern, however, you become aware of the choice that relates best to how you want to respond.

Ultimately, you have only one choice to make. Do you want to be proactive or reactive? In other words, do you want to be able to choose your responses in life? In the book *Reinventing Yourself: How to Become the Person You've Always Wanted to Be*, author Steve Chandler calls the ability to choose your responses *response-ability*, which is the best definition of that word that I have ever heard.

The Impact of Stress

Stress in one part of a system affects the other parts of the system. Think of a car engine. Suppose I keep revving up the engine until some part gives out. I replace that part with another, stronger part, but I continue to rev up the engine. Eventually some other part will give out.

Consider another example. Suppose that a large number of frogs in a particular area are dying. When biologists try to figure out why, they are likely find that there is some kind of stress in the ecosystem. Be it the fuel gauge on the space shuttle or the frogs in an ecosystem, stress in a system may initially manifest in one place, but it can easily affect the whole system.

Stress works in your family in the same way. Stress in one family member often shows up in another. Suppose you and Dad fight all the time, but you each go complain about one another to Mom. This stress is likely to manifest in Mom's health or state of mind. Just like the fatigue on the engine or the ecosystem, the stress has to come out somewhere.

When two people in conflict don't directly deal with the issues between them and vent to a third party to relieve the stress they feel, the situation is called *triangulation*. If this behavior is a pattern, the third party often feels the stress that exists between the two people in conflict.

KEYWORD: Triangulation occurs when two people in conflict complain to a third party instead of resolving the issue themselves.

Triangulation is an example of how everything affects everything else in a system. Your behavior affects everyone in the family and in the business. Likewise, everyone else's behavior will affect you. Once you realize this, you might choose to not put your stress on Mom and deal more directly with the issues you have with Dad. See how awareness creates better choices and better *response-ability?* Can you see why ownership for your attitudes and actions is important?

Think about the biggest sources of stress in your family. Can you sense where stress manifests? Can you look beyond the surface reasons for the stress and get to the root cause? Try to focus more on *why* something is happening or reoccurring rather than assessing blame or arguing about the details. If you make this shift, then you can move closer to realizing your part in the stress and deciding whether you want to act differently.

Play Your Part in the System

As part of a family and family business system, you should
- Look for patterns and realize they may represent a choice.
- Realize that all your thinking, choices, and behavior affect everyone else in the system.
- Have compassion for others in the system and the roles they play.
- Recognize that the roles people play usually help the system in some way.

The Complex Family Business System

In both your family system and family business system, the parts of the system are people. In the family, the parts are family members defined by their relationships. In a business, people are more defined by what they do, what they produce, and how much power they have. In the business, people's titles refer to their jobs, such as Chief Financial Officer; whereas, in a family, titles refer to relationships, brother, for example. As I explained in Chapter 1, the rules and purposes of these two systems are different, like the rules and purposes of respiratory and digestive systems are different. Yet both systems contain groups of people that are interdependent.

If a family is a bunch of people that creates a system and a business is the same, then how much more complex is the system known as the family business? Experts tell us that any system has to be more complex than its subsystems. For example, your digestive system cannot be more complicated than your whole body. Likewise, the family and the business are subsystems of the family business, which must be more complex than either.

In my consulting with family businesses, I am very fortunate to work with Steve Swartz, who has consulted in the family business field for more than 25 years. As consultants, Steve and I are committed to involving the whole family, even those who may not work in the business. Why? Because the family members and the family business are all connected. My mother, for example, never formally worked in my family's business. But did she feel involved? Did she have a sense of ownership? Did she influence decisions? You better believe she did, far more than some family members who were actually employed in the business. Ownership does not just mean legal ownership; emotional ownership or commitment is at least as important.

Many professionals become frustrated with family businesses because they don't realize that a family business is one big system that includes the family and the business. The two are interdependent, not independent. Any business or family business consultant who would have tried to help my family's business without understanding my mother's perspective or involvement would have missed a crucial part of our family business system. It would be like trying to clean up a river while ignoring the farmers dumping the fertilizer along the riverbanks.

Can you see why I and many other family business consultants use the systems perspective? It helps us move away from just the individual. We define a client not as any one person, not as the family or the business, but as the entire family business. Because everything affects everything, those consultants who deal only with a business issue, such as how much each of three related vice presidents should be paid, while ignoring the related family issues, such as the fact that these three siblings have a lifetime of being competitive, will miss a big part of the picture.

As the family business becomes more complex, involving more people, more roles, and more issues, planning becomes vital. Lack of planning, which relates to avoiding taking ownership, is one of the biggest reasons for failure in family businesses.

Sustainability

All living systems want to sustain themselves. Whether you are talking about an ecosystem, a family, or a family business, systems want to survive beyond the individual members. As part of a human system, you can decide whether to keep the system going. Human systems adapt to stress, to change, and to challenges, often without the people in the system thinking about how this adaptation occurs. Especially in families, people find ways of coping with things such as moving, illness, financial worries, and so on.

Most families, especially those working together in a business, need to work on making some of their automatic patterns into chosen behaviors. When I work with a family, I often remind the family members that they can do anything they want. I am just there to help them see whether their actions are getting them what they want. Family members need to step back, pause, and look at what they are doing to see whether their choices will lead them to the desired outcome. They need to see whether their choices lead to greater sustainability. For example, if Dad has six or eight drinks every night to deal with his financial stress, is that a sustainable path? As you look at your own behavior and see its consequences, you have the opportunity to make a choice.

Navigating Two or Three Roles

Roles are a context for who we are. We all act differently on a date than we do in a job interview, which is different than how we act in the classroom. Roles are important and necessary to function with people. Each role involves different rules and responsibilities. For example, you can be a very different person when you're with friends on a Saturday night than you are at work the following Monday morning. Your character may be the same, but your behavior will probably be different.

Think about your role in your family. Are you the responsible one? The funny one? The lost one? The black sheep? How is the way your family sees you different from the way your friends see you? Think of a role as a script. Imagine that you are a famous actor who is given a script, and you are deciding whether you want to play the part. (I encourage you to take this perspective with the role you play in your family or in your family business.) But you have even greater power than most actors do. If you don't like parts of the script, you can change your part. If you don't like being the irresponsible member of your family, you can decide to change your role.

How Does Your Role Benefit You?

Dr. Judy Provost (who has done some great work with the Myers-Briggs Type Indicator, especially as it relates to college-age people) has the notion that before you try to change your role, you should ask yourself how that role benefits you. This question is not always easy to answer. You might think, "I hate being the screwed-up one." But if you think about it, you are likely to realize that there was some reason why you fell into that role. For example, taking on that role may have helped the system, the group, or the family to sustain itself. Eventually that role may become destructive, but at the time you adopted it, it probably seemed appropriate.

Take the family scapegoat, for instance. A *scapegoat* is someone who takes on the troubles of the family. Why do people take on this role? They may do it, without being aware of it, to keep the rest of the family members feeling more comfortable about themselves. This role seems negative, because it enables everyone in the family to dump their frustrations onto one person. At the same time, it helps the other family members to avoid looking at their own problems and shortcomings. For example, I can more easily avoid looking at my fading interest in my career or my marriage if I have a brother who just got fired for punching his boss and arrested for driving under the influence. In this way, having a family scapegoat can help sustain the family system and benefit all of its members.

> **KEYWORD:** A **scapegoat** is a person in a family whose role it is to carry much of the blame and criticism. Focusing on the scapegoat helps the rest of the family members to avoid looking at their own issues.

A role is like a pattern in that it is a way of behaving that you can just fall into. Roles are broader, though, and may involve a number of patterns. For example, the role of scapegoat can include patterns of being late, irresponsible, and immature.

A role at one point in your life can be a wise choice, but as time passes that same role may not be wise or healthy. Again, ask yourself the question: When does this role benefit me, and when does it not? Even if you are the scapegoat, focus on why you have taken on that role instead of blaming others.

Which Role Are You Playing?

If you work in your family business, you have two very different roles to navigate: your family role and your employee role. Unlike people who don't work for relatives, those who work in a family business must continually be mindful of which role they are in. As David Bork describes in his book *Working with Family Businesses*, the situation is like owning one hat labeled *family* and one labeled *business* and having to constantly make sure you're wearing the right hat.

For example, calling your boss "Mom" in a board meeting might mix up the roles. As a result, you inadvertently encourage the other businesspeople in the board meeting to focus on your role as the son, not as the vice president. Or you might like being the clown in your family, but you probably don't want that role in the family business.

For another example of how these roles work, imagine that your parents are 55 and planning their estate. What should they do with their wealth? Their estate includes one million dollars in personal assets and 100 percent of the ownership of the family business, which is also worth one million dollars. They have three kids: you, crazy Ernie, and Fifi.

You have worked in the business for 12 years. Ernie dropped out of college his freshman year and has spent the last eight years sponging off your folks and surfing. Fifi is a gifted ballerina, but she's an anarchist who hates capitalism. Of the three of you, only Ernie is married, but his wife doesn't like the family, and your folks have never gotten used to having a tattoo artist in the family.

So of the two million dollars they have to divide, how do they do it as parents and as business owners? As parents, they probably want to treat their kids the same. We all whine if our folks don't treat us the same as our siblings, right? When it comes to divvying up the personal assets, that fairness makes sense.

But what about the family business assets? As business owners who want to sustain the business, your parents may need to talk with you if you are going to run the business. Could you run the business if Fifi, who would try to blow up this "capitalist empire," and crazy Ernie and his soon-to-be ex-wife each own a third of the stock? No, you would be a fool to try. To give the business the best shot of continuing, it would make sense for your parents to leave you a majority of the stock because you are actively involved in the business.

Perhaps you'll get all the stock while Fifi and Ernie each get what the stock is worth in cash. Because they would be entitled to about $666,000 each and the parent's personal assets of one million would only give them $500,000 each, you might have to sign an agreement to pay each of them $166,000 to even things out. Then again, your folks might set up trusts for the other two so they don't blow all the money on surfboard wax and black T-shirts! The important thing is that your parents clearly separate their family role as parents from their family business role as owners when they manage their assets. If you distinguish your family roles from your family business roles in your own life, you are far less likely to cause trouble, conflict, and confusion.

Preparing for Predictable Transitions

The interdependent relationships of families and family businesses change and evolve over time. As people who have studied individuals, families, and business have come to learn, these entities experience a fairly predictable series of transitions. How they go through the transitions varies, but the transitions themselves are fairly predictable.

According to the Small Business Administration, 40 percent of family businesses are facing *succession* at any given time (Raymond Institute/MassMutual, American Family Business Survey, 2003). Defined narrowly, succession refers to transferring the management of the business, but it can also include transferring the controlling ownership in the business or even the leadership in the family. You can broaden the term to include the following significant transitions:

- The new generation entering the business
- The ownership and governance passing to the next generation
- The family changing as a result of births, marriages, divorces, and deaths

With this broader definition of succession, how can a family business not be facing succession most of the time?

> **KEYWORD:** **Succession** is the way an organization continues to survive, especially related to leadership. Think of the shifts between U.S. presidents or Roman Catholic popes. In family business, succession concerns how to continue the family, the business leadership, and the ownership beyond the current generation. It is how a system lasts beyond the life of any one person.

Most family business consultants focus on the older generation's transition to the next generation. In my own courses and in this book, however, I have chosen to bring more focus to the transitions and challenges of the younger generation. Chapter 1 described the life stages of individuation and early adulthood. While you are experiencing these significant changes, your parents are going through their own changes. The family business has its own stages as well.

The Evolution of a Family Business

A successful multigenerational family-owned business goes through three major stages: entrepreneurial, managerial, and professional. Figure 3.1 provides an overview of how these three stages compare. As you read over the table and the description that follows it, think about which stage your family business is in. What are the transitions that you are most concerned about in the next five years?

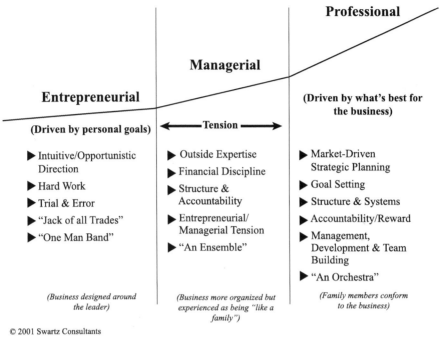

© 2001 Swartz Consultants

Figure 3.1 Stages of a Successful Multigenerational Family Owned Business

Note that in the entrepreneurial stage, the business is designed around the leader. If a business in this stage were a musical group, it would be a one-man band. Entrepreneurial businesses have an intuitive/opportunistic direction. Because they are often managed and owned by one person, they are flexible and can react quickly to opportunities.

Leaders of entrepreneurial businesses are forced to learn through their own experience of trying things until something works. They may have to learn to handle the accounting, finance, marketing, management, and technology of the business without being able to hire experts in these fields. Leaders of such businesses are usually extremely dedicated and willing to try to solve problems through sheer effort and time. In most cases, the business is their life.

A business in the managerial stage is more like an ensemble than a one-man band. In this stage, the business is usually larger than a business in the entrepreneurial stage and often has more than just the first generation of the family involved. Accordingly, it is more organized than a business in the entrepreneurial stage, but employees and management still experience it as being "like a family."

A business in the managerial stage must make many changes to accommodate its growth. First, the family business may have to hire some outside talent that the family may not have. For example, the first outside person hired is usually a financial expert. Additional management may be brought on board, thereby separating the ownership and management functions. As a result, budgets, audits, and spending controls become much more important. The business focus shifts from personalities to procedures, so such things as meetings, plans, and performance reviews are often implemented during this stage.

People from first generation may say things to the second generation like, "In the old days, we didn't need any plans and budgets." At the same time, the outside experts and advisors who have been hired are often suggesting the need for just such changes. What worked in the past for the first generation might not be working so well now.

The business in the professional stage is like an orchestra. This stage is characterized by substantial growth and often occurs when the family is beyond the second generation. In this stage, family members are conforming to the business instead of driving the business. The business has invested time, talent, and capital in certain business areas and now has to figure out the best way to take advantage of those niches.

In this stage, business owners must set the long-range vision for the business and hold management accountable for carrying out that vision. Everyone must be on the same page, so communication of this vision is important. Policies and procedures are in place so that issues such as hiring people, selling products, or talking with the media are handled in a consistent manner. Areas such as training are more formal. The business culture can no longer just flow from the personality of the founder or even the family. It has to be managed, and talent must be developed both individually and collectively. With plans, goals, and performance reviews in place, people have a clear sense of what they are expected to do, how they are doing, and what rewards (or punishment) they can expect to receive.

The Risk of Failure

Running a business is just plain hard, and your family members face some stiff risks as they decide to work together. The best estimates available indicate that only one out of three family businesses are still owned by the family in the second generation. So if you started out with 100 family businesses in generation one, you would have 33 family businesses in generation two. From the second to the third generation, about 11 out of the original 100 businesses would still be operated by the family. By generation four, only about three or four family businesses are left. Interestingly, the odds of success go up after generation four, probably because the family has figured out by then how to successfully keep the business in the family.

The one caveat is that a family not owning or operating the business is not always a failure. If the family plans to sell the business because the next generation, with the family's support, has decided to become artists or monks instead of business owners, then that cannot be called a failure. But this sort of scenario seldom happens. It is more likely that the eight challenges outlined in this book bring about a failure, and both the family and the family business suffer.

The two biggest reasons for family business failure are a lack of planning and inadequate preparation of the next generation. Most family businesses do not have a business plan, do not have a succession plan, and do not have a statement of why the family owns the business, often called a family constitution. Most families do not know how to prepare the next generation. A significant problem for the first generation is that the founders of a business usually have no one in the previous generations of the family from whom to learn.

I often hear the parents of my students say, "I really wanted to give my kids a better life, but somehow I feel they missed out on something." Your parents want to protect you from *unnecessary* suffering, yet they want you to gain credibility. (Remember, personal growth comes through personal struggle.) Dealing with life's adversities is what builds and defines character.

Once people in a family business realize how important it is to plan, they still don't do it. Why? There is often very strong emotional resistance—not just from the older generation, but also from everyone in the family and the family business—when it comes to planning and preparing for succession. This emotional resistance towards planning or preparing for the next generation is a huge problem, which is why Chapter 4 discusses this issue in detail.

Involving Your Family in This Journey

The process of taking control of your life needs to be your journey, which is why I put the ownership chapter before this one. Ultimately, you need to decide whether you want to take ownership for your life. You need to decide what you want to do even if your family never changes one iota. At the same time, you now know that you are part of this system called the family, and you may be a part or be deciding whether to become a part of the family business system. Either way, you have some affect on and are affected by the family business. You can make your own choices, but you are still connected to your family. Your family and your family's business affect you, and you affect them.

How do your involve your family in the process? The idea may seem paradoxical, but if you really want to bring about change in your family, the best way is to work on changing yourself. If you take the systems perspective, you will see why this statement is true. By changing yourself, you change your relationship to everyone else. By changing these relationships, you change the system that they define.

Set Rules for Communication

Don't set yourself up to merely play a role or perpetuate patterns. Look at your behavior and where it will lead. Also, as you do some reflecting on your life, your dreams, and your future inside or outside of the family business, I encourage you to talk to your family. One of the biggest benefits of the Stetson

University family business program comes from the students having up to a four-year discussion with their families.

Like the students at Stetson, you need to do two things to help make this process work. First, you need some space to reflect and discuss things. Your family may be too connected with you to let you just muse for a week about your dreams of rock stardom. It may be wiser to talk that dream over with a trusted friend or advisor. Second, you need to feel in control. It may be appropriate to set a boundary with your immediate family that you will talk with them every week or so. When you do talk to your family members, don't feel that you have to share every detail of your journey with them. Take ownership for how you process this journey by deciding when, where, and with whom you discuss your issues, dreams, and concerns.

Be mindful and compassionate, though. Realize that your family is concerned about you. They probably want to help, and they want to know what your plans are and how these plans are going to affect them. You can address these fears without disclosing everything. You may also want to make these topics part of an ongoing discussion with someone you trust. These discussions are a great opportunity to apply what you will learn in Chapter 5 about applied intelligence.

Seek Outside Assistance

Just like professional athletes have trainers, psychologists, and doctors to help them, you might benefit from finding some help with your family issues. A psychologist is involved with the Family Enterprise Program at Stetson, and my colleagues and I refer people to the campus counseling center fairly often. If some issue comes up that seems overwhelming or about which you feel you cannot talk even with a close friend, then seek professional help from a therapist.

I see so many people with the attitude, "I would go if I really needed it." But I can't tell you how many students come in to my office during their first semester and say, "I hate my roommate, I am failing my classes, I am afraid my parents are going to be disappointed, and I am so stressed out that I just can't handle it." I usually suggest that they talk to someone at the counseling center because the therapists there have helped many students deal with this exact transition. Almost all of the students say the same thing. "Well, it's not *that* bad."

I challenge you not to think of therapists as people you see only when it gets "*that* bad," but as people you see whenever it might help. I am amazed by the people who will gladly pay someone to teach them how to swing a golf club, cook dinner, or exercise, but never consider hiring a professional to help them with some of life's bigger issues. For example, if you were having a hard time dealing with the grief of losing a loved one, do you think a therapist who has helped 400 people deal with this issue could help you? You might say, "It's not *that* bad," but I would ask, "Would it help?" Keep this topic in mind as you read the next chapter on emotional resistance.

Focus on Making Progress

This book asks you to take ownership for your life. How much are you willing to practice what you have learned? This process ain't easy. You might feel this way the first day at the gym with a fitness trainer. Remember, your goal should be progress, not perfection.

If you are feeling at all overwhelmed, take a deep breath and pause for a minute. Try to take it one step at a time. A good stress management technique is to break down projects that seem overwhelming into manageable pieces. I would recommend you consider applying that idea to this process. Commit to an amount of time, such as two hours each week, to reading and practicing the ideas in this book.

Conclusion

The first three chapters in this book have given you a lot to think about and likely a new perspective on things. This is powerful and profound stuff. The next chapter examines another reason that taking ownership of your life is so difficult: emotional resistance. This sneaky, subtle force can be a helpful red flag in some cases, but far too often it keeps you stuck and adds to the suffering in your life and the lives of people you love.

As you go through the rest of the book, keep in mind what you learned in this chapter:

- The parts of a system are interdependent. As a result, stress or change in one part of the system affects everything else in the system.
- A human system is made up of people and the relationships that connect those people. The family and the business are subsystems of the more complex human system of the family business.
- You should be aware of which system you are participating in at any given moment and what your role is in that system. This awareness can help you maintain credibility and analyze how your role benefits the system.
- Recognizing which stage your family's business is in will help you and your family plan for the business's future and increase the odds that the business will successfully pass on to the next generation.
- The choices you make affect your family just as the choices your family members make affect you. Because you are so connected to your family, you may find it useful to find a friend or another person outside of the family business system to talk to about the life decisions you are considering.

CHAPTER 4

Overcoming Emotional Resistance

T his chapter begins to connect the process of growing up, becoming your own person, and taking ownership for your life with the challenges that lie ahead for you. If making this connection were merely a matter of me explaining these challenges and rationally convincing you that you need to address them because you will be better off, then the work would be pretty easy. But there is more to it. Before you can address the challenges, you must overcome a big obstacle, and that obstacle is emotional resistance.

This chapter is about dealing with your emotional resistance, and it is the most important chapter in this book (and the longest). If you don't understand this chapter, then much of the value of this book will be lost.

By the end of this chapter, you will be able to

- Understand what emotional resistance is and how it works.
- Identify the defenses and red flags that signal emotional resistance in your life.
- Realize why emotional resistance is a poor way to make decisions and how it keeps you from attaining what you really want.
- Start to deal with your emotional resistance.

Understanding Emotional Resistance

In 2001, I attended the Third Annual Friends of the Center for Creative Leadership Conference in Kansas City, Missouri. While I was there, I listened to a wonderful speaker, a man many people consider to be a true guru among business consultants, Peter Block. (Many people recommended his book, *Flawless Consulting*, which I found fascinating.) Block noted that clients often are resistant to a consultant's help. (Note that Block labels this idea resistance, whereas I prefer the more specific term *emotional resistance*.)

Why would someone hire you to help him, and then resist your efforts to do so? The answer is that the person feels vulnerable. At least on some level, the client has said, "I can't do this, and I need help." For some people, that is tantamount to admitting failure. I have found resistance to being vulnerable with a consultant to be even more prevalent when the client is a family business. In those cases, the vulnerability relates not only to the business, but to the client's family as well. That is a delicate situation.

We all fight against feeling vulnerable by using defenses that separate us from our fears. This reaction is what I call *emotional resistance*. Emotional resistance typically operates outside our awareness, at least at first. It serves us, in that it seems to protect us from emotional discomfort. However, it fails us as a way to make decisions. That distinction is very important.

> **KEYWORD:** **Emotional resistance** is the struggle against feeling vulnerable. Underneath your emotional resistance often lies true insight.

How Emotional Resistance Works

So what does emotional resistance mean if you are between the ages of 15 and 25? Think of the transitions you are undergoing, a big decision you have to make, or a project you need to complete. Emotional resistance blocks you from taking the action you need to take, whether it is deciding on your major at college, breaking up with the biker dude or goth girl you're currently dating, or talking with your dad about joining the family business.

For example, you may not want to decide on your college major because considering your choices reminds you that you could pick the wrong major, fail, waste those four years, end up in a career you hate, become a homeless person, and cause the downfall of civilization as we know it. (Okay, so I got carried away. You get the idea.) You may not want to dump the biker dude because you don't want to hurt him. You also may be putting off talking with your dad about joining the family business because you are afraid of being judged or even rejected. Emotional resistance may show up in many different forms, but essentially it is about avoiding looking at what is really going on inside yourself.

Why You Need to Deal with Emotional Resistance

Not everyone is aware of emotional resistance, but everyone has it. Just as a fish is surrounded by water, we are likewise often immersed in our own emotional resistance. Not dealing with your emotional resistance keeps you from realizing what you really want (the true insight I referred to previously), and you can't get what you want if you don't even know what it is.

Remember that beneath emotional resistance lies vulnerability. You must get to that place of awareness that exists beneath your emotional resistance, to that place of vulnerability. That place will tell you what you are truly feeling and will help you see what you really want. Otherwise, you are stuck, repeatedly trying to deal with the surface issue and never facing the real issue.

Suppose you have a short in the wiring in your home that keeps burning out the lightbulbs. If you deal only with the surface symptoms by repeatedly replacing the lightbulbs, then you will become frustrated; waste a lot of time, energy, and lightbulbs; and never get to the underlying cause. Find the underlying cause, and you can fix the problem and get back to the rest of your life.

Don't let your underlying problem gradually worsen until it does you significant harm. You need to able to recognize when you are demonstrating emotional resistance and then learn how to push past it to discover the underlying issue or problem that you are avoiding. Figure 4.1 shows this process.

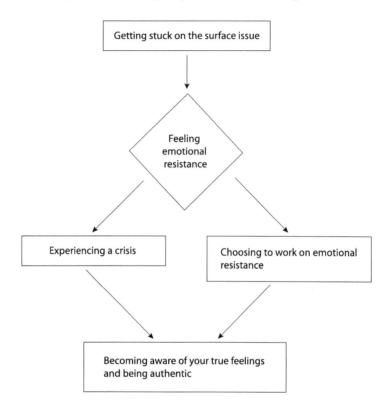

Figure 4.1 The different levels of handling emotional resistance.

When you get stuck on the surface issue, you are not dealing with your emotional resistance. Instead you use defenses, such as avoidance, humor, intellectualizing, minimizing, and procrastination. You also focus on what your symptoms are and who is to blame for things not going your way. However, your analysis of the surface issue doesn't seem to help. You feel stuck and find yourself repeating patterns, yet you still think the solution to your problem is for other people to change the way they behave.

When you begin to feel your emotional resistance, you are in a constant state of tension because you are afraid of being vulnerable. You can move out of this stage by crisis or by choice. Although a crisis may get you unstuck and drive you to be vulnerable, the stress of the crisis is likely to make it hard to act wisely from your new awareness. A better way to move out of this level is to work on being aware and working with what is going on in your life so that you, not the emotional resistance, do the deciding. Useful tools in this work include attention, patience, support, feedback, and advice.

When you move beyond analysis of the surface issue and uncover the underlying cause of your emotional resistance, you can be authentic. You can break out of your patterns and become aware of your choices. For example, you can choose how to act, what to communicate, and how much to trust the other people involved. You are not waiting for other people to change because you have decided to change yourself.

Remember watching yourself on video for the first time and saying, "Do I really look and sound like that?" It took some time to get comfortable with seeing yourself from a different perspective. Likewise, dealing with emotional resistance is a process that takes some time to get used to.

Most people initially react to someone pointing out their emotional resistance with disbelief and denial. A friend of mine was struggling with her life and went to see a priest, a doctor, and a psychologist. All three of them said that she seemed very angry. I had lunch with her, and she just couldn't believe their reactions. She did not see herself as an angry person. After she spent some time reflecting on that idea, however, she came to realize that she really was angry. That is the tricky trait of emotional resistance; you almost never see it at first. Give it time and think about asking a friend for some feedback on the areas where you feel stuck.

Recognizing Defenses

You know you have emotional resistance when you catch yourself using defenses. Defenses are ways of thinking or behaving that protect you from being vulnerable. Although defenses are the ways that your emotional resistance manifests itself, they are not the emotional resistance itself. Just like your body reacts to fear with an increased heart rate, greater focus, and heightened senses, your emotional self expresses emotional resistance through defenses. Just as greater focus and heightened senses can be useful traits to have in some situations, defenses can be useful tools when you choose them.

The following are some typical defenses:

- **Minimizing**. *It's no big deal if I don't do well in school. My dad says I already know more than his top guys.*
- **Intellectualizing**. *If only 5 percent of adults have written life plans and a lot of them do fine, then I don't think it is worth my time to do any planning. Besides, things change too often to plan.*
- **Avoidance and procrastination**. *I have just been so busy, but I will get to it if everyone would just stop bugging me about it.* Of course, you find that anything takes priority over the thing you've been avoiding.
- **Humor**. *Aw, I don't need a plan. I can get by with my charm and good looks!* This statement is always said with a grin and usually a twinkle in the eye.
- **Denial**. *Yeah, my boyfriend seems to be getting the message. Sure, he just sent me a dozen roses for Valentine's Day, but I think he knows it's really over.* This one is amazing; the person using it just refuses to accept that the issue even exists. Students often use this defense when graduation is looming and they haven't made a career plan. They act as though someone else might be looking out for their futures.
- **Bodily signs**. These signs aren't defenses, but they can be red flags for your emotional resistance. Do you get headaches, stomach problems, neck or back tension, or even sleeplessness because of stress? These symptoms may indicate that you are not dealing with your emotional resistance.

Which ones are your favorites? Mine tend to be humor, intellectualizing, and minimizing. As you confront big or stressful decisions, just watch how these defenses appear.

Using Your Defenses

Typically defenses operate without you being aware that you are using them, and that is the problem. When you use defenses unconsciously, you allow them to make the decisions and run the show. As a result, instead of addressing the underlying fear, you just avoid dealing with it. Avoidance doesn't make the fear go away, but it does make you and others around you feel stressed. Remember from Chapter 3 what stress does in a family system?

When you use your defenses more consciously, you can decide when they help you and when they harm you. From that increased awareness, you can make better choices. The following sections show examples of how you might use your defenses.

Putting Off a Major Decision

Suppose you can't decide on your college major. You keep telling yourself that this decision isn't that important because you are only a sophomore, and you know a guy who didn't figure it out until his senior year.

In this situation, you are using both procrastination and minimizing. Procrastinating on choosing a major only makes it harder to select one and less likely that you will graduate on time, especially if you haven't even started assessing the choices. That guy you knew who didn't decide on a major until senior year had to take extra courses, do an independent study, stay an extra summer, and suffer a lowered GPA. He also ended up taking courses he didn't need or want. Those two history courses he hated but took because they were the only ones available at noon didn't count at all toward the marketing major that he finally chose.

To be fair, procrastination does have its benefits. First, you are more flexible and open to new information when you put off making decisions. The person who decides early on that he wants to be an accounting major and sticks to it in spite of finding out that finance makes more sense is not necessarily better off than the procrastinator. Second, the procrastinator may stumble onto the major she really wants through her rambling, spontaneous, and unstructured path.

However, these benefits are all by luck; they are never intentional. Furthermore, you risk never developing the ability to self-assess, to clarify what success means for you, and to take ownership for your future. I would raise Dr. Judy Provost's question from Chapter 3 here: When does procrastination benefit you, and when does it not? Do you want to continue to procrastinate because it benefits you or because you don't want to deal with the underlying vulnerability? Is your emotional resistance to starting the search or to making a commitment to one major? In a nutshell, *why* are you procrastinating?

Some students can be working on a plan, keeping their options open, and still collecting more information about themselves. They may not have made a final decision on a major. Does that style work for you? For some people, that flexibility and openness is best for them. For others, it is just a way to avoid committing. This distinction is subtle. The process of overcoming emotional resistance is more about being honest with yourself than making a decision.

Taking the Romance out of Romance

What if you know the biker dude (or goth girl) you've been dating isn't right for you, but you don't want to hurt him (or her) by breaking up the relationship? You might think to yourself, "I just won't talk to him. He'll get the message." That's called avoidance.

Now perhaps your avoidance and silence benefits you in that the other person may begin to realize that the relationship is over. But she is going to fear the worst—not only that the relationship is over, but also that it ended because of whichever trait she is most insecure about: her height, her weight, or her unusual rash. (Of course, when you finally decide to tell her that you don't want to date her anymore, you may or may not decide to be totally honest about the reason.) In this case, your silence has added to the person's suffering as he or she agonizes over whether the relationship is over.

When you try to deal with your emotional resistance instead of staying on the surface level of this issue, you may realize that you are not protecting the other person's feelings with your avoidance. In fact, you are trying to protect yourself from feeling like the bad guy. You can avoid dealing with your feelings and having the break-up conversation for only so long, and while you are avoiding it, neither of you can start to move on to a better relationship. You are both probably feeling a lot of stress from feeling stuck. Not a great place to be, huh? If you want to be authentic, it's time to choose an approach that serves you and the other person for whom you once cared.

Discussing Career Plans with Dad

You have thought about the possibility of joining your dad in the family business after you graduate from college, but you have not discussed your thoughts with anybody in the family or the business. You say to yourself, "I'm not sure what I want to do at graduation, so I'll just wait and see what happens." You think it is not very important to talk about this topic with your dad while you are still in school.

By not discussing your career plans with your dad, you are missing out on discussions that could inform your actions for the next few years. For instance, should you take some courses in marketing or management? What type of internship would be best? More generally, what are the skills, credentials, and experiences your dad, *as head of the company*, would like to see you have at graduation that would help you enter the company with credibility?

Not having the discussions might enable you to avoid the possibility of being criticized or even rejected by your dad, but staying at the surface level comes at a cost. You aren't going to be able to verify your assumptions. (Remember my story from Chapter 1 about the student whose dad told him he was going to sell the business within the next year?) Does Dad want you to join him? What position would you fill? Does Dad think you have the skills to do it? Does he believe in you? Does he think you need to have outside work experience first? Does that prospect scare you because you have terrible grades so far? On the other hand, if you do not want to join the family business, is he going to say he needs you or that you owe it to the family to join the business? Without having the discussion, you can't make informed plans about your future. Is your decision to not have these discussions truly benefiting you or your dad? Or is it a way to avoid dealing with emotional resistance?

Facing Family Business Issues

Let's shift to something more immediate and see how your emotional resistance might play out in your use of the book *When Your Parents Sign the Paychecks*. You might say, "Oh, I can do this stuff in my head. I don't need to write out my goals or talk with anybody about family business issues." That's intellectualizing. It's akin to saying that you'll never pick up a bat before playing in the big baseball game because you think that sitting on the couch watching old World Series tapes is enough preparation. Or you might think, "Heck, no one ever follows the suggestions in the book." Could you be minimizing? How about this comment: "I will do the work. First, I just want to read the book." That's either procrastination or avoidance.

Pause, take a deep breath, and decide whether you want to develop beyond where you are now. Consider what happens in situations where you let your emotional resistance make decisions for you. Think about what happens when you make decisions at the surface level of dealing with emotional resistance instead of the authentic level. When these things happen, you are prone to get stuck in a place where you feel a lot of stress. You are going to feel as if you keep having the same argument, finding yourself in the same circumstances, or trying to analyze your way out of the surface issue—and none of these approaches ever seem to work!

Confronting Your Fears

Emotional resistance prevents you from looking at, dealing with, and starting to overcome your fears. It undermines your credibility, and it is a painful place to get stuck. The only way to address your emotional resistance and start to move beyond it is to commit to looking at what is behind the emotional resistance and facing this underlying fear.

Here are some typical fears that just may be the underlying cause of your emotional resistance:

- **Fear of failure.** *If I really take ownership of my life, I might fail.* Realize that if emotional resistance prevents your progress, you are destined to fail.

- **Fear of success.** *If I succeed, then others will expect more of me in the future.* It's true that successful people have to deal with the pressure of high expectations. But isn't this pressure preferable to others having no expectations of you? Or worse yet, having no expectations for yourself?

- **Fear of committing.** *If I never really try, then I will never really fail.* Avoiding a decision may feel safe, but so many people don't understand that not deciding is a decision, and it is a poor one.

- **Fear of disappointing your parents.** *It would break my dad's heart if I worked for another company instead of the family business.* Your parents want you to be happy, and if you are trying to achieve that, almost all parents will be happy. Beyond that, you have to decide whether being authentic is important to you. If it is, you will have to confront this fear.

- **Fear of disappointing others.** *If I don't go with all my friends to an internship in Chicago, they might all hate me.* This fear is similar to the last one, but it plays out with friends, mentors, colleagues, and bosses. It is a real and understandable fear, but you need to look at it more deeply to determine what pleasing others costs you and to question the assumption that you know what they want. Remember that you are responsible for your own happiness.

Ultimately, you want to move to a position where you are making a conscious choice about what you want and how you want to act. You make the decision rather than letting your emotional resistance make it for you.

Being Vulnerable

Recall that the underlying issue beneath the emotional resistance is the fear of being vulnerable. That makes sense, right? Who likes to be vulnerable? However, I said that you need to face this fear in order to overcome your emotional resistance. However, realize that facing your vulnerability doesn't mean that you have to expose your vulnerability to others. If you expose your vulnerability to other people, you risk getting hurt. By simply being aware of your vulnerability, you have done the work to overcome your own emotional resistance, yet you still can choose and use defenses.

Using a defense is like being able to pick up a shield. If it truly shields you from hurt, using it is a good, healthy, and wise choice. But if you use the defense simply to strengthen your emotional resistance and avoid dealing with your fears, then it is destructive and unhealthy. The key to protecting yourself is to use defenses purposefully instead of unconsciously.

Protecting Yourself

Suppose that you are going to see mean old Aunt Erma. She is a nasty woman who always picks on you, never has anything nice to say, and knows how to push your buttons. You have to go see her about a getting a letter of recommendation for college because you worked for her last summer.

You reflect that you almost always end up arguing with Aunt Erma because you feel attacked. You feel stuck in this pattern with her. You realize that underneath your emotional resistance is a fear of being criticized. To avoid feeling vulnerable with Aunt Erma, you choose to use your defenses to protect yourself.

You might just avoid going to see her and try to get away with an e-mail request or getting your dad to ask her for the letter (avoidance). If you decide to go ahead with the visit, you might mentally prepare by talking to yourself ahead of time to about how she is always mean and how she will focus on all the negatives about you and blow them out of proportion (intellectualizing). Once you are at her house, you might try to deflect her criticism. If she says you were always late to the job, you might say, "Well, at least I excelled at something (humor)." After you leave feeling beat up, you might realize that this is only one person's opinion. Most people in your life see a lot more positives in you than the alphabetical list of negatives good old Aunt Erma just gave you (humor on my part, minimizing on your part).

There are two important things to note in this scenario. First, Aunt Erma is someone that it makes sense not to be vulnerable with (I never did like her), so you are consciously choosing to use your defenses. Second, you are aware of your emotional resistance. You are still choosing to overcome your emotional resistance to feeling vulnerable *with yourself*, and you are still clear on how you feel and what you want.

There's no reason to be vulnerable with other people when doing so serves no purpose or is not wise. For example, it is unwise to be vulnerable with someone who has a history of trying to attack you, in a formal setting such as a job interview, or when you are overly tired.

Choosing to Be Vulnerable

There's a difference between when you recognize your own vulnerability and when you choose to share that vulnerability with another person. Opening up about certain topics with certain people might be inappropriate, but it is always appropriate to be open with yourself. If you can't be vulnerable with yourself, whom can you be vulnerable with?

You may well decide to be vulnerable with another person even when it is not entirely safe. For example, you might decide to tell Aunt Erma how her behavior hurts you. You may decide to be open with your dad about your fears even if that means risking that he will not make you a job offer.

When you are considering any issue concerning emotional resistance, you should first get clear about how you feel on your own, perhaps by initially talking with someone who does not have an emotional investment in the outcome. If, after processing your feelings, you decide the heavy metal band is your career path instead of the family business, then that discussion is one to have with your parents, even if it is not entirely safe.

In closing, the real risk in vulnerability comes from not being vulnerable at all. A life spent trying to avoid vulnerability is a wasted life. The poet Ranier Maria Rilke said ultimately it is our vulnerability upon which we depend. I think he meant that what emerges from our vulnerability is our insight into how to be who we really are, connect with people we love, and uncover a path for our life. It is the place a truly individuated person goes when making important decisions.

Making Decisions Without Emotional Resistance

Remember that emotional resistance serves you in that it can protect you from emotional discomfort, but it fails you as a way to make decisions. It hinders you from dealing with your underlying fear or vulnerability, which eventually leaves you feeling stuck and stressed. In short, using your emotional resistance to make major life decisions is like using your airbag to drive your car. It is the wrong tool for the job and never gets you where you where you want to go.

The following sections address the issues and provide examples of pushing through emotional resistance to make decisions that are in line with who you truly are. This process is hard work, but doing the work is much better than dealing with the stress that comes if you don't.

Handling the Stress of Emotional Resistance

Consider an example of emotional resistance in your life. Where do you feel stuck, as though you're having the same discussion or argument over and over again? What tough decision are you not able to resolve? Think about that issue. Pause. Don't try to change anything. Just watch what comes up. Which of the emotional resistance red flags, your defenses, starts flapping in the breeze? As I mentioned earlier, consider how using your defenses benefits you. Does it protect you from being vulnerable? If so, what are you vulnerable about?

Assume that as you reflect on this issue, you realize that if you let your emotional resistance make the decision about whether to work and apply this material to your life, then you are definitely not going to do the work because you are going to feel vulnerable. But you know what? Vulnerability is what it takes. Remember, personal growth comes through personal struggle. Do you want to look at the underlying fear or suffer the stress of not dealing with it? If you stay stuck, the problem is apt to become a pattern.

As explained in the section "Why You Need to Deal with Emotional Resistance," there are only two ways to get to the authentic level: by crisis or by choice. Of course, you can wait until life throws you a crisis. In my mind, however, waiting on a crisis and then reacting is like waiting until you have your first heart attack before you start working out. It is better than nothing, but far from the ideal way to live.

One of my favorite quotes is from Roman statesman and philosopher Lucius Annaeus Seneca, "The fates lead him who will; he who won't, they drag." I believe this quote means that either you deal with an issue or it keeps getting worse and worse until it causes a crisis or so much trouble you can no longer ignore it.

When you are middle-aged or old, do you want to look back at the big decisions and transitions of your life and say that you really dealt with them? Or do you want to feel like your entire life has been an accumulation of the stress and consequences of not dealing with your emotional resistance? If you want a recipe for being unhappy and being a victim, emotional resistance is the way to go!

Doing the Hard Work

Can you find the discipline to be vulnerable with yourself, step up to the plate, and take ownership for your future? The biggest difference between people who take ownership for their lives and people who do not is the way in which they work with their emotional resistance.

Talent can only take you so far, and emotional resistance can derail anyone's progress because it never makes a good decision. In some ways, I think people with great talent or intellect often can go longer in life avoiding some of this work. However, the longer they wait, the harder it is to deal with their issues. It is like getting in shape. You may think it is hard at 20, but, man, it is a lot tougher at 45. Just ask your folks.

Dealing with your emotional resistance is hard, but the reward is profound. I will also tell you an encouraging truth. Although confronting the fears underlying your emotional resistance can be tough at first, it gets easier the more you do it. Recognize that the deep, reflective thinking that this process requires takes time, but this is time well spent. It's better to take the process slow and steady than to overdo it and burn out. Strike a balance between not pushing too hard and not giving up.

Planning and Emotional Resistance

I gave a talk at a national convention where I spoke with about 60 owners of family businesses. Only one had a business plan, and not a one had a succession plan. I believe all of them knew they should have these plans, so why didn't they? The answer is emotional resistance. In my opinion, it's just that simple—simple, but not easy.

Planning is hard, and I think it makes people feel vulnerable. For example, a succession plan requires people of the older generation to consider their own deaths, and that is a big area of vulnerability for just about everyone. Even business planning asks people to commit to a plan of action, create accountability, and share that plan with other people, which also creates vulnerability. In my classes, I have students complete the McCann Action Plan for Life. Invariably, students will say that writing about who they are and where they want to go brings up fears of failure, success, and criticism. Planning for your future usually triggers emotional resistance.

Ask your parents if they have a business plan or a succession plan. If they don't, ask them why and listen to the answer. (Remember, discretion is the better part of valor, so take a moment to reflect before you rush off to confront your parents right after you finish reading this chapter.) Their answer may help you see firsthand how hard it is to overcome emotional resistance and start to plan.

Making Authentic Decisions

I had a student who was reluctant to go to graduate school. As we talked about it, he explained that his uncle had given a lot of money to the school, and he felt he might be admitted just because of that. Also, his uncle had done well as a student at that school, and he didn't want to compete with that legacy. (By the way, neatly categorizing emotional resistance is sometimes tough, but I would call his emotional resistance intellectualizing and avoidance. Would you?)

On the surface, these sounded like good reasons. But after talking to me for a while, he admitted he was really afraid of failing. He knew that graduate school would challenge him to give his best. Although he might succeed, he might fail for the first time in his life, so he felt vulnerable. When we talked about his fear of failure, he was able to examine it and decide on graduate school based on something other than the surface issues. I admired his willingness to open up to a trusted advisor and take ownership for his emotional resistance.

Ultimately, he decided to go to graduate school. But in this situation, the important thing wasn't whether he went to graduate school; it was whether he made the decision based on his emotional resistance or his core values. He didn't let emotional resistance make his decisions for him, and neither should you.

Working with Emotional Resistance

This book is not just an argument about why you should take ownership for your life, but it is also a guide for how to do it. An important aspect of taking ownership is dealing with your emotional resistance. You can choose to go from the surface level of dealing with emotional resistance to the authentic level, but remember that courage is the necessary starting point. Most people wait till the fates drag them to face their emotional resistance. Think about whether you have the fortitude and courage to choose to work on your emotional resistance and move forward.

When you decide to deal with your emotional resistance, you can use the following tools to help you:

Awareness
Attention
Patience
Advice

Support

Feedback

Benchmarks

The following sections describe each of these tools.

Awareness

The first tool is awareness. If you aren't aware of your emotional resistance in general or specifically concerning the issue at hand, then you can't deal with it. Awareness takes time to cultivate. The key to being aware is recognizing when you are using defenses, which is a major signal of emotional resistance. Another signal is your body showing signs of stress.

When you feel stuck, go back to the description of the surface level of dealing with emotional resistance in the section, "Why You Need to Deal with Emotional Resistance." Does any of this description sound familiar? Are you waiting for the other person to change? Do you feel like you have been in this situation before? Can see your defenses coming out?

Once you become aware of emotional resistance, however, it is hard to ever be unaware again. If you want to maximize your personal growth, then help your friends to become aware of it, too. This way, you will be able to confront one another about emotional resistance, although not in a harsh way. In my experience, when people are in the company of others who help them feel it is safe to look at their vulnerability, that makes it easier to do. If you feel that you are going to be judged, attacked, or ridiculed, you are far less likely to open up and look at yourself. Remember, ideally vulnerability is a choice.

When you start dealing with emotional resistance, make sure you apply yourself to your problem before you start calling other people on their emotional resistance. They may not be interested in working on their emotional resistance or ready to do the work. You should serve as an example of how to work with emotional resistance instead of a preacher telling others what they should do. Besides, focusing on someone else's emotional resistance is just another way to not look at yours (otherwise known as the avoidance defense).

Attention

Emotional resistance is a little like a child that is crying—sometimes all it wants is attention. One curious thing about emotional resistance is that if you pay attention to it, it lessens. Pay attention to the evidence of your emotional resistance, your defenses. Before you try to change them, judge them, or criticize yourself about them, just pay attention to them.

Watch what you are saying to yourself. "Oh, I will do it later." "It doesn't matter." "Only a nerd would do this." "It won't make a difference." Again, don't try to fix it, don't beat yourself up, and don't even act on it yet. Just pay attention to the resistance with the intent of getting to the underlying fear.

Are you using humor, but no one is laughing? Are you procrastinating and feeling the stress and pressure building? Try to pause and think about and feel what it going on. If you can label the type of defense you're using or the fear you're feeling, then that may help you to start to deal with your emotional resistance. Keep in mind that this kind of attention takes time and practice to develop.

Patience

Do you really want to deal with an issue by letting your emotional resistance decide? Take time to think about that question. Don't be in a hurry to act on any insight you have gained. Be patient and allow yourself some time to reflect. You may learn something about yourself.

After you have reached the authentic level of dealing with your emotional resistance, let the dust settle. Keep the focus on yourself and how you are feeling and thinking. Acting can almost always wait. I'll tell you something most people don't learn until later in life: Processing life's big issues by learning how to be silent, reflective, and available is a much better way to engage life than by simply avoiding the tough decisions.

Advice, Support, and Feedback

Taking ownership for your life does not mean that you do not want and need to seek support. In the program at Stetson, the students and I talk about emotional resistance issues one day a week in an hour-long class. Not only does that help the students realize that other people deal with similar issues, but also committing to take an action in front of others puts some positive pressure on the students to do it. I recommend asking people for help when you need it.

Of course, when you ask people for help, you need to frame your request carefully so that you ask for what you want. Do you need advice, support, or feedback? In class, I use an exaggerated example to explain the difference between these tools. If your foot is caught in a train track and a train is bearing down on you, you want my *advice* about how to get the darn foot out. *Support* would be bad at this point. Imagine if I said to you as the train is coming down the tracks, "You know, I had this happen to me once and I want to share how I felt with you. I really understand what you are going through." That would be the wrong tool at the wrong time. If you put your foot in a train track on a dare, then maybe a few days after the event, when the stress has passed, I may feel the need to give you some critical *feedback* on the impact of that behavior.

> **KEYWORD:** **Advice** is a suggestion about a possible solution to a problem. **Support** is validating another person's feelings without judgment or criticism. **Feedback** is an analysis and opinion about a specific behavior.

Before you ask for advice from someone, consider your mindset. Pause and think about what would help you. If you are overwhelmed, stressed, or confused, support is likely to be the most helpful. Getting some of that stress off your chest tends to help you feel more available for feedback or advice. It is hard to strategize about solutions when you feel as if you are on the verge of losing it. When you are ready for advice, ask someone whom you respect and who has some experience and expertise that relates to your problem.

An important part of becoming a professional is getting feedback from the people you work with so that you can improve your performance and learn how others perceive you. Suppose you have to lead a meeting, make a sales presentation, interview a client, or terminate an employee for the first time. You probably want a trusted advisor to observe you and tell you what you did well in these situations and what you might consider changing. Such an advisor can see things that might be difficult for you to see on your own.

When people you work with offer an opinion of your work, listen to them. You may just gain some valuable insight about how others perceive you. When my students, the audience members from speeches I give, or my consulting clients give me feedback, I usually question them and draw them out to get more concrete feedback. If their perception of me differs from my own, I explore those differences.

When you ask for feedback, consider whether you want to focus on improving your skills or understanding how others see you. The kind of feedback you will receive depends on the person you ask. For example, when I give a speech, I might ask someone I know to be a great speaker for feedback about my speaking style, whereas I might ask the head of the trade association I am speaking to for feedback to check whether I met her expectations.

Sometimes you will be in the position to use advice, support, and feedback to help somebody else instead of asking for help. Recognizing which tool is most needed in a situation helps you to become a better friend, family member, and professional. Of the three tools, advice is the one that is most often misused. For example, guys typically give advice almost automatically whether people ask for it or not.

Advice is most useful if you have actual experience with this type of problem and the person asks you for advice. Even then, realize that each problem has a degree of uniqueness to it, so your advice may not always fit. Advice can be a real pain to someone who doesn't want it, so make sure the other person is open to it before you offer it. Ask permission before you give advice. Otherwise, it is like trying to pour water into a pot with the lid still on. It does no good and makes a mess.

Many people automatically give advice when they hear a friend or family member talk about a problem. But if your best friend just found out she is failing all her classes only an hour after her boyfriend dumped her, she doesn't want a to-do list of advice from you. She would probably prefer support. Support is acknowledging the other person's feelings by saying, for example, "That must be hard" or "I am sorry that it didn't work out." Unlike advice and feedback, support is never judgmental or critical.

Feedback is ideally given either when someone asks for it or you feel the need to give it. For example, if your friend has been dumped by her last seven boyfriends, all of whom say she is too clingy, you may feel the need to give her some feedback on that pattern of behavior.

There are three parts to giving feedback. First, you tell the person in a calm, objective manner the behavior you saw, such as, "Friday at the orientation meeting you introduced yourself to me." Then, you tell the person the affect of that behavior on you (or others), "I felt glad that someone was nice enough to break the ice." Third, tell the person what specifically you would like. "I would like you to continue that behavior with me and other people in this organization," for example. When you give feedback, keep in mind this guideline established by the Center for Creative Leadership: When giving feedback, you should give four positive comments to someone for every critical comment.

When you are giving advice or feedback, remember one thing. As Peter Block notes in his book *Flawless Consulting*, realize that you can never, ever overcome emotional resistance with a rational argument. Imagine your best friend is deathly afraid of spiders, and you have flown in a dozen of the world's top spider experts to convince her that the spider that you want to have crawl on her is perfectly harmless. Think it is going to work? If all I had to do to get a family business to act was to give them a convincing, rational argument, my life would be much easier. But it ain't that easy. Don't argue with yourself or anyone else about emotional resistance, or you are very likely to lose.

Benchmarks

Another tool for dealing with emotional resistance is the benchmark, which can help you break tough tasks down into smaller and more manageable steps. Instead of saying you will complete this book by sunrise and cure cancer by the weekend, just say that by Monday you will work through this chapter and talk it over with someone you trust as an advisor. Those small manageable goals help you feel as if you are making progress, gaining momentum, and succeeding.

Finally, let me give you one last technique. Commit to regularly devoting a certain amount of time to this process. When I was writing this book, I would commit to working on it a certain number of hours (typically two) each day. I have a lot of emotional resistance around writing, but far less around my teaching. I tend to find writing difficult because it feels like teaching to an empty room. To motivate myself to write, I had to look at the fear of failing to finish the book or letting people down, which is that a big fear for me. Setting aside a certain amount of time each day for the project made it easier to work with my emotional resistance.

Conclusion

If you have made it through this chapter, the toughest of the introductory chapters, give yourself credit. This material is not easy stuff. I will also tell you a secret. My core value is working with people who want to work. That tends to mean I am a tad demanding, but I think that good teachers *are* demanding. As I tell my students, I believe in you and I expect more from you than you might think you can handle. I believe you have the potential to be a professional, to take ownership for your life, and to learn how to work with your emotional resistance. Now that you've worked through this chapter, I hope that you feel the same way.

Dealing with emotional resistance is the threshold for the remaining chapters. If you are willing to deal with your emotional resistance, you should feel good about your ability to confront and overcome the challenges ahead. Keep these thoughts from this chapter in mind as you go forward:

- Emotional resistance is a person's fight against feeling vulnerable. The vulnerability stems from such fears as the fear of failure and the fear of disappointing others.
- Defenses such as procrastination, denial, and intellectualizing are signals of emotional resistance. They can also be protection against people to whom you don't want to show your vulnerability.
- Not dealing with your emotional resistance results in stress and puts you in a poor place from which to make decisions.
- Dealing with emotional resistance is a difficult process. Give yourself time to assess what you are feeling and thinking and to figure out why you are feeling and thinking that way. Don't be afraid to ask others for help in the form of advice, support, or feedback.
- Remember that underneath your vulnerability lies insight and the wisdom of your authentic self. Discovering this authentic self is one of the greatest rewards for the hard work of personal growth.

PART II

Meeting the Lifelong Challenges in a Family Business

P art II examines the first two family business challenges, which are challenges that you will have to confront for the rest of your life. Chapter 5 deals with a concept that will likely be new to you: Applied Intelligence. This concept is similar to the idea of emotional intelligence that has been popularized by Daniel Goleman. Emotional intelligence is the concept of taking responsibility for your emotions. Applied Intelligence is the practice of making sure that your behavior conveys your true character and that your reputation and character align.

The second lifelong challenge, which is dealt with in Chapter 6, is managing wealth. Money has many meanings in families, especially those that own businesses. Control and cash are almost always issues that need to be addressed with my family business clients. For members of the next generation, wealth can be a force for growth or a source of corruption.

CHAPTER 5

Challenge 1: Improving Your Applied Intelligence

My father, Norm McCann, tells the story of an employee who had a power lunch with potential investors at a very expensive restaurant in New York City. The employee ordered french fries, which he ate with his fingers, licking off the salt and oil between bites. The investors didn't notice the employee's qualifications and ample knowledge of his business. They only noticed his horrible table manners and opted not to invest in the company.

Close your eyes for a moment and think back to high school. Remember the smartest kids in your class, like the chess champion and valedictorian. Would you want to be friends with all of them today? Would you hire them to work in your family's business? Even though these people were all competent and intelligent, I would bet that in some cases you would want to keep your distance.

Both of these examples describe people with low Applied Intelligence. Applied Intelligence is probably a new term to you. For this book, having Applied

Intelligence means choosing to take ownership of your character and deciding how you want to behave toward others.

After reading this chapter, you will be able to

- Understand what Applied Intelligence means.
- Improve your Applied Intelligence by applying a six-step process.
- Analyze the remaining seven family business challenges in terms of Applied Intelligence.

Defining Applied Intelligence

You may have heard of emotional intelligence, a concept developed by psychologist Daniel Goleman. Emotional intelligence refers to the ability to manage your emotions. Applied Intelligence is different. It's more focused on understanding your behavior and taking responsibility for it. My father presented this idea of Applied Intelligence in a talk with my students about 12 years ago.

Applied Intelligence is the awareness that your behavior affects how people act toward you. Applied Intelligence is not impression management, nor is it a way to manipulate, trick, or appease people; it is behaving in a way that reflects your character.

> **KEYWORD:** Applied Intelligence is the practice of mindfully aligning your behavior (and therefore your reputation) with your true character.

You consist of your internal character and your external behavior. Your character reflects your true self, which includes your intellectual, moral, and emotional qualities. Your behavior, on the other hand, determines how others perceive you. After all, everyone knows that observing a person's actions is a better way to assess a person than merely listening to what the person says. These perceptions determine how people act toward you and are reflected in your reputation. As shown in Figure 5.1, Applied Intelligence bridges the gap between your true self and your reputation.

Applied Intelligence: A Framework

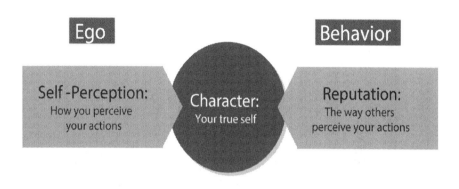

Figure 5.1 The role of Applied Intelligence.

Competence Is Not Enough

My father used to open his talk to my students saying, "You have been led down the wrong path." This statement was his way of saying that students have all been terribly misled about what it takes to be successful. How? While you are in school, more than 80 percent of your success is determined by your technical competence, and less than 20 percent is determined by Applied Intelligence. Even if you offend the teacher and everyone in the class, you will probably get an A if you score well on the exams. Beginning the day you graduate, however, that equation reverses itself. On the job, about 80 percent of your success is determined by your Applied Intelligence and only 20 percent is determined by your technical competence—but no one tells you this!

In your professional career, you need to be technically competent; you need to master what you do. The shift from high school and college is that in the business world the "what" accounts for only about 20 percent of your success. How you do things makes up the other 80 percent of why you succeed (see Figure 5.2). So even if you are technically the smartest person in the firm, you may not succeed if you are late, rude, unethical, or even have poor table manners. You need to master both the what and the how, yet your formal education has focused only on the what.

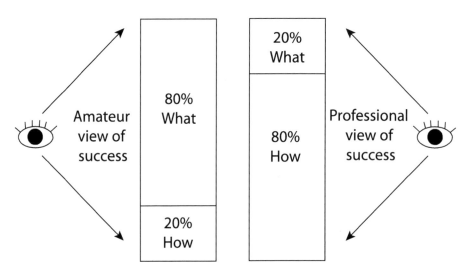

Figure 5.2 Two perspectives on success.

In fact, far too often college unintentionally reinforces the notion that being right makes up for being offensive. (Think back to the smart classmates I asked you about at the beginning of this chapter.) Most people believe that if they are technically competent or "right," then they ought to succeed or at least be rewarded for their knowledge and abilities. In my experience, such a belief is the single biggest cause of career derailment, especially in a family business. Certainly, competence is important, yet I have never encountered a single individual who was fired solely for technical incompetence. Competence is your ticket to the game, but it doesn't guarantee a win.

If you feel that because you are technically competent you don't have to be concerned about the rest of your behavior, then you are expressing a sense of entitlement. Chapter 7 details the risks in having a sense of entitlement, but for now, just know that such an attitude can be very destructive. Essentially, you are saying that you don't have to take ownership for your behavior because you are right or have a certain amount of skill. If you think about it, you'll realize that almost everyone thinks he is right, even the person who disagrees with you!

People who succeed are distinguished from the others not by their "rightness" or technical competence, but by the areas of behavior relating to Applied Intelligence. These areas include the following:

- **Attitude.** Are you proactive or just reactive? Are you a mostly positive or mostly negative person? Do you take ownership for your behavior or do you always make excuses? Proactive, positive people who take responsibility for their actions demonstrate a high level of Applied Intelligence.

- **Attire**. Think of your clothing as part of your nonverbal communication. What do your clothes and appearance say about you? Does your appearance show that you are a professional? Does it align with your character? Do your clothes, hygiene, and general appearance enhance your credibility? Don't mistake being flashy for appearing professional. Getting dressed to go to a club is very different from getting dressed for work.

- **Communication style**. Can people tell where you stand? Being too introverted or too extraverted can leave others guessing what you are really thinking. Are you polite, articulate, clear, and concise? Do you convey criticism in private and regularly give out praise in public? These actions are the mark of a socially intelligent person.

- **Ethics.** Do you do the right thing even when you don't have to, when you think no one is watching, or when it comes at a cost? If so, then you are demonstrating that you are someone who is willing to invest in your character and reputation. You are someone people can trust.

- **Manners.** By using good manners, you convey that not only are you a professional, but that you also are mindful of how you treat others.

- **Empathy.** This quality is the core of Applied Intelligence. Can you step outside of your own needs and be aware of other peoples' feelings, needs, and concerns? This ability is vital to how you do everything!

Focus on the First Impression

People make an overall assessment of you in less than a minute, and that first impression starts to solidify very quickly. Consider what factors you use to assess others. Research shows that over 90 percent of the characteristics by which people assess others are body language, attire, and behaviors. Notice that none of these has to do with what people say.

Appearance does matter. I once ran a discussion of a group of about 10 men and women who made hiring decisions in professional firms. I asked if there were a typical error that interviewees make that would disqualify them even before they sit down or open their mouths. They all agreed that dirty or scuffed shoes would eliminate the candidate. So if you think you are technically competent, take time to reflect on what first impression you make, and polish those shoes!

Others' Perceptions Affect Your Reality

My father would tell students, "Other people's perceptions of you create your reality." I would say it a little less dramatically, perhaps, but this statement expresses the core concept behind the principle of Applied Intelligence. How someone sees you affects your reality because people treat you based on how they perceive you and your reputation.

Seeing yourself as others see you can be difficult and maybe even shocking. (If you've ever watched yourself on video, you know what I mean.) However, in order to develop Applied Intelligence, you must learn how to see yourself through others' eyes.

Suppose you are 25 years old and have just been hired by your family's business as vice president of sales. You worked in sales for three years after graduating from college, and you believe you are up to the challenge and are as qualified as the two other vice presidents. However, the other two vice presidents are 36 and 40 and have at least 10 years of experience. They also both worked for outside firms for at least five years.

You have always been a fairly quiet person. You find small talk somewhat awkward, if not downright phony. During your first week on the job, you head into the company cafeteria to eat lunch alone. Some employees you have met in the past say hello, and one of them asks you to have lunch with them. Given your introversion, the pressure you feel to get up to speed in the new position, and your attitude toward small talk, you decide having lunch and chatting with coworkers isn't a priority this week. You reply by grumbling about wanting to look over some work and being too busy to eat with them.

Step back and try to look at this situation from your coworkers' point of view. What perception have you created? What reputation are you building? In your situation, some coworkers are bound to perceive that you were given this position just because you are a family member. Add that perception to the apparent aloof behavior at lunch, and you probably have a reputation for being arrogant and a bit of a snob.

Perhaps if you were not a family member, other employees' perceptions might be less critical and certainly would not affect the reputation of the family and the family business as directly. If you weren't carrying the weight of the family's power with you, your coworkers might be more likely to simply perceive you as a quiet guy. But the fact that you are a family member contributes to their perceptions of your behavior. As a result, although you may not intend to seem aloof, and "arrogant snob" may not describe your true character, that has become your reality at work.

Imagine that at the end of your first week you go to the eight employees working for you and ask them to help you out by coming in to work on a Saturday. You get a cold reaction. They have plans on Saturday, they want to put it off until later, or they otherwise resist. Suppose one of them, your uncle, knows you well and is secure in his job. He pulls you aside and says perhaps you started off on the wrong foot. Your uncle knows you, but the other seven people can only act on their perceptions from your behavior during this first week on the job. Although a request such as yours is pretty typical in this firm, many of your coworkers complained to your uncle about your aloof behavior.

One of them, the guy who asked you to lunch, even told your uncle, "He can't even say hi to me, and I am supposed to give up an entire Saturday for him? No way!"

After your uncle's calm recounting of the facts, you are shocked and even hurt to discover people perceive you as a snob. You see that your coworkers' perceptions create your reputation, even if their opinion conflicts with your true character. Your reputation is worse than you think you deserve, and it has nothing to do with your qualifications.

If you are like most people, your initial reaction to this realization is to lapse into the "Yeah, but..." syndrome. "Yeah, but I just don't like small talk." "Yeah, but I am kind of shy." "Yeah, but they need to understand that I am under pressure to get up to speed." If you pause and reflect on this issue, though, you will see that you are requiring other people to somehow look beyond your behavior and realize what your true character is.

Your uncle might say, "Sure, once people really get to know you, they will realize that their first impression isn't really who you are. But I am concerned about the reputation you are creating." Unfortunately, people in all areas of your life, particularly in business, don't have the time to withhold their assessments until they "really get to know you." As the saying goes, you never get a second chance to make that first impression.

The Struggle for Applied Intelligence

In Rocky III (1982), Sylvester Stallone portrays Rocky Balboa as he struggles to confront his lack of Applied Intelligence. In this movie, Rocky has won the title of heavyweight world champion, and he believes he earned the title. However, he finds out otherwise—his trainer, who is like a father to Rocky, has been picking easy fights for him to protect him from getting hurt. This situation sounds a little like protective and well-intended parents trying to protect their son or daughter from failing in the family business, doesn't it?

Shortly after his trainer reveals the truth, Rocky loses the title fight, and his trainer dies. Rocky has to face the fact that his reputation and his character are very far apart. People view him as washed up, unwilling to earn the title and unable to defend it. Of course, if you have seen any of the Rocky movies, you know what must happen. With help from the one person who believes in him, Apollo Creed, Rocky strives to win back his credibility and recover the "eye of the tiger." See, even Rocky needs support in his battle to improve his Applied Intelligence!

Improving Your Applied Intelligence in Six Steps

To help you start thinking about your own Applied Intelligence, consider these questions:

- Did you wear scuffed shoes to your last job interview?
- Has it been a long time since you sent a handwritten thank-you card to someone and not just an e-mail?
- Has it been a long time since you sincerely apologized to someone?
- Have you ever yelled or cursed at a server when there was a problem with your meal?
- Do you excessively use the word "like" when you are talking?

If you answered yes to any of these questions, your Applied Intelligence could use some improvement. Improving Applied Intelligence usually involves changing your behavior to better reflect your internal character. After all, changing your external behavior is much easier than changing your internal character.

Improving Applied Intelligence is a six-step process:

1. Consider which role(s) you want to examine. Are you acting as a family member, an employee, or an owner?
2. Pick a behavior to focus on. It can be a neutral behavior (such as quietness)

or a troublesome one (such as chronic tardiness). If nothing leaps to mind, then pick one of the following behaviors that is most applicable to you: extroverted or introverted; impersonal or sensitive; impatient or laidback; detail oriented or big picture oriented.

3. Step back and look at the perception that behavior can create in others.
4. Analyze whether this perception conveys your true character.
5. Determine how that perception creates your reality: How do other people treat you because of it?
6. Decide what adjustments you want to make, and then make them.

Relating Applied Intelligence to Different Roles

To be effective in a family business, you have to navigate the three different roles or "hats" discussed in Chapter 1: family member, employee or potential employee, and owner or potential owner. So how does Applied Intelligence relate to managing these three roles?

If you work in a family business, you may switch roles often throughout the day. For example, you might have breakfast with Ernie as his spouse at 7:00 a.m., then join him at 8 a.m. for a staff meeting as his boss, then catch him up at the 5 p.m. owners' meeting, and finally, back in your role as spouse, crawl into bed with him at 10 p.m. You have navigated three roles with the same person in one busy day with various people watching, assessing, and creating their perception of you, the family, and the business.

In Chapter 3, I said family members, owners, and employees have different rules and responsibilities. Your character plays out differently within these roles. Consider these questions:

- What family rules aren't appropriate in your business role?
- What business rules aren't appropriate in your family role?

Start with the first step of realizing which role you are playing, whether you're in your family, employment, or ownership role. In the earlier company cafeteria example, you were a family member, but acting in your employee role.

The role of family member can sometimes be tricky when a family business is involved. Imagine you go into the family business to pick up some books you lent to your younger sister Sarah. You don't work there, but Sarah is the office manager. She has worked there for only two years and has to manage people who have been there for many years, who are older than her, and who have known her since she was five years old. Like many big brothers, you enjoy teasing your baby sister. You notice she is wearing a short skirt. You don't really think it is too short, but in front of some of the employees you say, "Hey, Sis! Want me to run by the house and pick up the rest of that skirt?"

What do you think? Was your behavior appropriate? (If you imagine Sarah standing over the shredder with your books, you are on target!) Even if the skirt was too short and you were technically correct, it was not kind to say it in front of the other employees. Doing so hurt Sarah's feelings and her credibility, and it may have even shortened your life span.

How about your role as an owner in your family business? Suppose that you own 10 percent of the company, you are a family member, and you have just started working in the sales department. All your peers in that department are identified on their business cards as sales associate. You, however, insist on having your business card read *owner*.

While operating as an employee, you are reminding everyone that you own a part of the company. Others might perceive that you're broadcasting, "Don't forget that I am not just a sales associate. I own part of this place, too." At best, they will perceive you as naïve. At worst, they will perceive you as arrogant. Because you are an owner, your coworkers might be afraid of you and resentful. The sales manager might be slower to give you objective feedback, and the sales team might be slower to invite you to go out for a beer after work. Your behavior is separating you from the rest of the group, and the other people in the group are likely to respond by keeping their distance from you.

Does the perception that your coworkers have of you in this case align with your true character? If so, leave it alone. My hope, however, is that it doesn't.

You may want to rethink your business cards and change them to read *sales associate* like the others in your department.

Viewing Your Behavior from Another Perspective

Step two of the six-step process of improving your Applied Intelligence is to pick a behavior and focus on it. Suppose you want to focus on your introversion. Consider how the behavior serves you. How does it help? When does it help?

Follow step three and step back and imagine what perception this behavior creates in other people (this is an example of using empathy), especially those who may not know you well. Often in a family business system, everything affects everything else, so you may want to consider how that behavior is perceived by the family, the other employees (both family and especially nonfamily), and even owners. As you saw earlier with the hypothetical introverted vice president of sales, such behavior can create a perception of aloofness or snobbery among employees, especially nonfamily employees who have never met you before.

Because seeing yourself objectively and getting beyond defenses is so hard, getting honest feedback from others about your actions is vital. Getting feedback from other people in the family and the business is good, but I also recommend getting feedback from trusted outsiders, because it is far easier for them to be objective when they have no stake in the game.

Conveying Your Character

Step four is to consider whether you are conveying your true character through your actions. This step requires letting go of or going beyond any defensiveness you feel about your behavior. (This may be a time to go back to Chapter 4 and review the material on emotional resistance.) You need to clearly identify your true character. Who are you? What do you stand for, and what you will not stand for? When does this behavior not work for you? Before you read this chapter, did this behavior seem like a good choice? Does it still?

The challenge here is not to defend your behavior, but to step back and see it from the other person's point of view, and then choose what you want to do. This step requires you to realize that you bear the responsibility for the consequences of your behavior. Ask yourself whether your behavior, in the role you are in (family member, employee, or owner), aligns with your character. You may decide that although your behavior has potentially negative consequences, you feel it is in line with your true character. For example, you might stand up for the environment, or you might confront a superior about his drinking on the job. That action might have potentially negative career consequences, but it can still be socially intelligent.

The fifth step is to look at how the perception you created with your behavior affects the behavior of others, how their perception of you will create or at least affect your reality. How are they going to treat you?

If you were focusing on your introversion and the behavior described in earlier example, you would recognize that eating alone and ignoring your colleagues undermined your ability to foster teamwork and goodwill among your team until your odds of getting these people to voluntarily give up a Saturday for you were pretty slim. Maybe you could order them to work on the weekend, but perhaps the culture of your family's business holds that it is best to get people to volunteer. Besides, they all feel as if they have credibility in the firm, and you don't—at least not yet.

On the other hand, if your trait is chronic tardiness, you may find that people see you as unreliable, as disrespectful of their time, and incapable of managing your own schedule. Through your lateness, you may erode their trust of you, your reputation, and your overall credibility. In contrast, you may see yourself as a trustworthy but overscheduled person, but remember that this step is not about defending your behavior; it is about stepping back and using your empathy to understand the perception your behavior might be creating.

Changing and Explaining Your Behavior

Now that you have an awareness of your behavior and see that you have choices, how do you want to change your response? The sixth step is to assess what realignments you want to make. Sometimes you just need to explain your behavior to others. In other cases, you may decide it is necessary to change your behavior.

My father says, "Silence, when communication is expected, will never be interpreted positively." If Applied Intelligence is being aware of what perception your behavior creates, then realize that silence when people expect communication will create a negative perception and result in damaging your reputation. So tell people what is going on! Watch your emotional resistance, too, because we are all prone to say we are avoiding communication in order to save another person's feelings, when in reality we are just trying to save our own.

Often when I go consult with a family business, the family members tell me that there's an issue about which they don't want to talk to their employees. Yet in virtually every case, the employees are at least aware of the issue, and they are almost always imagining the worst. Communicating even bad news is better than to let their fears run rampant and their perceptions run amok. In such cases, silence becomes a giant screen onto which other people can project their greatest fears.

Consider a conversation that would go a long way toward remedying your situation as the vice president of sales in the lunchroom. Imagine you had called all your direct reports in the first day and told them you are totally committed to showing everyone you have earned this job. Your family may have afforded you this opportunity, but you know you will have to work hard to truly earn the right to maintain your position. You also told them that you tend to be an introverted person, and socializing doesn't come easy to you. After this first week of training, however, you would like to have lunch with each of these seven direct reports over the next month. You asked for their understanding, help, support, and patience, especially during this first week when you're trying to get your footing. Wouldn't that talk have created a very different perception and reaction to your request for them to volunteer to work on a Saturday?

Along with communicating to others and helping them understand your actions better, you might also want to adjust your behavior. Maybe you could work on initiating conversations, getting to appointments on time, and so on. If you're a strong introvert, for example, you can start conversations by asking questions, set agendas for meetings so you can feel more ready to speak, and label your silence. For example, you might say that you want a minute to think about something or even that you would like to take the weekend to reflect on that idea. Once you become aware that the message you have been conveying does not connect with your values and character, you can choose to reframe your message in the future.

Ideally, you will be able to involve other people in the practice of Applied Intelligence. Practicing Applied Intelligence is like keeping up a good exercise routine—most people benefit from the support and positive pressure others give them to keep at it.

Cultivate Applied Intelligence

You can improve your Applied Intelligence by following these tips:

- Express gratitude often. Buy a box of thank-you notes and send at least one a week. (E-mail doesn't count.)
- Treat others' time as very important. If you are going to be late, call as soon as you can and follow up with an apology, not an excuse.
- Don't leave people hanging. At the very least, tell them when you will get back to them.
- Remember that it is sometimes better to be kind than to be right.

The Three Players Practice Applied Intelligence

A simple example of Applied Intelligence (or the lack thereof) that I see often at school is when a student misses a week of class because he or she was sick. All too often, the student does not contact the professor or ask any of the other students in the class what he or she missed. At issue in this example is the behavior involved in handling a class absence and interacting with a college professor.

Suppose that Professor Strickland has outlined in the course syllabus three things students should do if they miss class: get an excuse from a doctor or health services, write a page on the assigned reading and turn it in the first day back (yep, that means today), and e-mail the professor to schedule a time to go over what was missed.

In the introduction to this book, I described three family business players: Tony, the amateur; Selina, the semipro; and Pat, the professional. Let's see how each of them might handle this situation. Note that I analyze their responses in terms of three points: their emotional resistance, their family's expectations, and their Applied Intelligence. I use this three-point analysis on the players in the rest of the challenge chapters in the book as well.

 ### The Amateur

On Tony's first day back, he goes up to the professor after the class is over and says, "Hey, I was sick. What did I miss?" Meanwhile, four other students are standing around waiting to talk with the professor. What perception of Tony do you think the professor (the guy who took the time to write a syllabus) has now? The professor is likely to think, "This guy is a slacker who doesn't follow directions, doesn't accept responsibility, and is more than willing to take advantage of my time." Do you think that perception will help Tony when he wants to miss class for a family trip later in the semester, change his scheduled time to take the final, or ask for a letter of recommendation? Do you think Tony should retool his behavior or just whine that mean old Professor Strickland just ain't cool? (In fact, that is what he told his parents.)

On the three-point analysis, Tony comes up short. He has not dealt with his own emotional resistance to accepting his responsibility as a college student. Given that he has taken this approach with a professor, it seems as though his family encourages his attitude of entitlement. (If you remember from the introduction, he told one of his parents' employees to type a term paper for him last semester.) His Applied Intelligence is a big risk because he can easily be perceived as a tad arrogant and self-centered.

The Semipro

Selina read the syllabus and has both the written assignment and a doctor's note. She forgot to e-mail the professor, so she stops by right before class to ask him if they should meet. The professor is on his way to class and seems a tad annoyed, but he is glad that she has her homework and note. However, she forgot to copy the note and asks Professor Strickland if he could copy it and return the original to her (and thus learns that apparently the professor's dream in life was to teach, not make copies for his students). Strickland sees that she is trying. He isn't overly impressed, but he is glad that she is more responsible than Tony.

Selina has apparently overcome the emotional resistance to seeing that handling school absences is her responsibility. Her family's expectations are unclear in this case (but that is likely to come up in a later chapter). In terms of her Applied Intelligence, she conveys the attitude of someone who is trying but is not yet totally competent.

The Professional

Pat e-mailed the assignment and the request for a meeting to Professor Strickland and left a copy of the doctor's note under his door with a note on it referencing her e-mail to him. She also obtained two classmates' notes, and based on those notes and her own reading of the material, she included some questions that she would like to discuss in their meeting in her e-mail to the professor. The e-mail also explains that she had left a voice mail with his departmental secretary saying that she would be out sick for a few days, which he is able to verify later. (The secretary forgot to pass along the message.)

Professor Strickland feels like his time is being respected, and he will gladly help Pat learn the material that she has questions about. He did sign up to teach after all, not to make copies for his students. He is impressed and would be more likely to accommodate Pat on missing class for a family vacation, rescheduling her final, or writing a letter of recommendation for her. He is impressed when Pat sends him a handwritten thank-you note a week later for reviewing what she missed.

Pat has overcome her emotional resistance to being an independent college student and sees handling an absence as completely her responsibility. Her family already sees her as more independent. She has decided not to seek advice on issues like this from her parents, but has found a mentor in a senior who lives in her dorm. In terms of Applied Intelligence, she conveys that she is competent, proactive, and mindful of people's time. In short, she is professional.

Conclusion

Since I started teaching (and applying) Applied Intelligence, it has shaped not just the family business curriculum, but also the behavior of students and many of my colleagues. Why? I believe that learning about Applied Intelligence lends you an opportunity for greater integrity, in the sense that your behavior aligns with your character and values. Ideally, your behavior also aligns with the values of your family and the family business.

Improved Applied Intelligence also affords you the opportunity of greater success. By success, I mean the conventional external definition measured by accomplishments and respect. I also mean success as I have defined it in this book, which is working in a manner that aligns with and expresses your values.

For more than a decade, I have discussed Applied Intelligence with people ranging from 18-year-old freshmen to tenured faculty to 80-year-old CEOs. Although I believe it is insightful, it is intellectually a pretty simple concept. The value, and the difficulty, comes from applying it. If you think you have mastered Applied Intelligence, go ask three friends, family members, or coworkers to read this chapter and give you some honest feedback about three areas where you deserve praise and three areas you might improve.

One semester, early in the term, all my students initially ranked themselves either above or way above average on their Applied Intelligence. By the end most had shifted to "average," not because their behavior had changed, but because their *awareness* had shifted. Give yourself time to learn.

Remember the highlights from this chapter:

- Applied Intelligence is the practice of aligning your behavior with your character. It requires you to cultivate empathy for others.

- Most of your success in business is determined by your Applied Intelligence, not your technical competence.

- Others' perception of your behavior affects how they act toward you, so you should always be aware of how you are being perceived.

- In a family business, you should always clarify what your role is in a situation before you act.

- Sometimes you need to explain the reasons for your behavior to others. Silence when communication is expected will always be interpreted negatively.

- Applied Intelligence is an important factor in meeting all the challenges relating to a family business.

CHAPTER 6

Challenge 2: Handling Wealth and Power

I remember once consulting with a client on the second day of a series of family meetings. After years of struggling to keep the business going, the family members suddenly realized that they were now all very wealthy. Different members of the family had been somewhat aware of this fact to varying degrees, but this meeting seemed to be the first time they had talked about it together. If you could've put one voice to those five family members it might have said, "Wow, this is great, but oh my God, what do I do now?" The wealth had given them freedom to do whatever they wanted, and they were happy about that, but at the same time, they felt great stress about how to figure out what to do with that freedom. Surprising how wealth can create such stress, isn't it?

So what does wealth mean for you and how can this chapter help? By the end of this chapter, you will be able to

- Appreciate how wealth can be a benefit and a burden for you and for others.
- Understand and begin to apply the concepts of commitment, stewardship, and human capital.
- Connect all of this information about wealth to your efforts to develop credibility and marketability.

The Challenge of Wealth

Wealth is a complex thing. It can represent access to power, freedom, and opportunity. In a family, it can be a way that emotional issues play out. For anyone, but especially for young people in a family business, wealth carries a profound risk of undermining your success and happiness. The challenge is to learn how to handle wealth and the related power while not being corrupted by it. The challenge is to have the discipline to continue to test your mettle and to still stick to your values and face consequences of your behavior, even when you have the freedom not to.

Ultimately you have to commit to something in your life. Most people, such as my clients for much of their history, never have to struggle with this challenge because they simply have to commit to paying their bills. Because they have to commit to *some* job in order to survive economically, they never are forced to address what they chose to commit to and what they really want out of life.

Wealth takes away that pressure of having to survive, but it leaves you to more directly face the pressure of deciding what you want to commit to. The challenge is that if you do not have that immediate economic pressure, you are likely to lack the discipline to ever figure out what you want to commit to (and often even with the pressure you may not find out what you really want, but more about that in Chapters 8 and 9). Don't let wealth keep you from taking ownership for your life and committing to a career path that brings meaning to your life and others' lives. Don't let wealth *corrupt* you.

KEYWORD: In this context, being **corrupt** means letting wealth and power influence you to the point where you act in a way that does not align with your values and erodes your credibility. For example, your parents give so much money to the college you attend that you can get away with things none of the other students can, and you take advantage of this fact even though you feel guilty about it. Corruption is when you let wealth prevent you from taking ownership for your life.

Life Without the Struggle

Studies of people who won the lottery show that one year after they win they are no happier than they were beforehand. (These studies were described in the article "Lottery Winners and Accident Victims: Is Happiness Relative?" by P. Brickman, D. Coates, and R. Janoff-Bulman, that was published in the *Journal of Personality and Social Psychology*, August 1978, volume 36, pages 917-27.) When I mention these studies in my classes, almost all of my students say that if they won the lottery, it would be different for them. But consider for a moment why it might be just as true for you.

If you are wealthy at a young age, an age when you are figuring out your identity, the wealth can very easily enable you to avoid the personal struggle involved in becoming your own person. Without the struggle, you will never find your true identity. It takes extraordinary discipline to make this journey voluntarily without the financial pressure most people feel. That is one of the great burdens of wealth, especially wealth that you have before you have figured out who you want to be. Money can make it too easy to avoid the journey necessary to figure it all out.

If you are in a burning building, your life becomes focused on one difficult but very straightforward goal: Get out of the building. If you have to pay the bills at the end of the week, your life may be similarly difficult but uncomplicated. Simply, you need a job to pay the bills. If you, like my clients mentioned previously, now have the means to do anything you want, then your life is (at least arguably) good and perhaps even easy in a sense. However, it also has now become very complex. You don't have to worry about paying the bills, so your job can fulfill the other goals you have in your life. Of course, you have to figure out what those other goals are. To meet this challenge takes discipline, vision, values, and an attitude of ownership (really stewardship, but more about that idea later in the chapter).

The Benefits and Burdens

I once met with a young man whose father was worth about one billion dollars. The father owned a car collection, two planes, a jet, and an impressive estate.

The son had some very nice toys as well. The young man and I talked for a while about his future, his interests, and his concerns. I told him that the one thing his father's money could not buy him was his own sense of credibility. He said, "I know!" He knew that his father's wealth would allow him to do anything he wanted, but he was unsure how to figure out what he wanted, not unlike my clients mentioned at the beginning of this chapter. He also seemed stressed about how to figure it all out.

Over the years in my roles as director, professor, and consultant, I have met many next generation members from wealthy families. Though virtually everyone envies them, such wealth does come with its own set of benefits and burdens. I have seen some of these young people, often with their parents' support, use their wealth and power to avoid the legitimate consequences of their behavior. Sometimes that means getting the dean to extend deadlines, getting the boss to not hold them to the same standards as other employees, or even just having parents who don't hold them accountable.

At the extreme, this kind of treatment cultivates an attitude of not just entitlement, but that any shortcoming is not their fault. So they often feel that they don't have to look at anything, work on anything, or take ownership for anything. (Remember that this extreme risk of wealth and power is by no means applicable to all or even the majority of the next generation from wealthy families.) These young people have taught me how having a lot of money can be a burden, especially at a young age. Some of them may have been much better off without it.

The Truth About Being Rich

If you get a chance, see **Born Rich**, a documentary that aired on HBO. The film was made by Jamie Johnson of the family that owns Johnson & Johnson, and it may change the way you look at being the next generation from a very wealthy family. In the film, Jamie interviews other heirs to large family fortunes, including the Trump and Vanderbilt families.

When I saw the film, I was sad to hear these young people talk about how the subject of money was such a strong taboo in their family, how they became millionaires without ever earning any of the wealth, how they feel alienated from friends because of their money, and how little they knew about their family and the history of its business. To me, the most powerful statement in the film came when one of the heirs talked about taking two years away from college to work as a laborer in an oil field. For the first time, he realized hard work made him happy. He learned that you have to test your mettle—a lifetime vacation won't make you happy.

The Recipe for a Happy Life

Many people, especially those who are younger, think that a life with no responsibilities and a lot of money is the recipe for a happy life. Yet when I have met people from families that own businesses or families of great wealth who have never had to grow up and never have forged their character through hard work and the related successes and failures, they have, without exception, been miserable. A wise colleague of mine who is about a generation older often says, "Things don't make you happy." I have come to appreciate that statement.

I know an impressive, educated, and thoughtful woman whose family business was sold, giving her the economic ability to never have to work again. But as she said to me, "You still have to figure out what you want to do when you get up each day." In other words, you still need to find out what you want to do and what you want to commit to in your life. If you think you can be happy without testing yourself and finding your own path in life, you are wrong.

Most people want to feel as though they are giving something back to the world. The opportunity of wealth is that you can do this on a larger scale. For example, Bill Gates created the Bill and Melinda Gates Foundation with family members to help the world, and with the recent gigantic contribution from Warren Buffet, the sky is the limit for what this foundation can accomplish.

Consumers and Stewards

Wouldn't it be tragic if your family business beat the odds and survived from your parents' generation to yours (only about a third do) and the end result was that all your folks' hard work and sacrifice merely lead to your being a spoiled adult with an attitude of entitlement and no real identity? The starting point for working with wealth and power is your attitude. You have to decide whether you are a consumer of wealth or a steward of it and how valuable human capital is to you.

Keep in mind that that you will most likely pass on your attitude toward wealth to your kids, and your deeds will speak louder than your words when you become a role model for your children. Do you really want them to become spoiled adults?

Completion by Consumption

If you see money and power as just ways for you to get what you want, you are setting yourself up to misuse the wealth and the power it brings. Folks who have this attitude are often looking for what writer Mark Epstein, in his book *Open to Desire*, calls "completion by consumption." This is the notion that you can deal with your sense of lacking and your emotional insecurities and even avoid searching for your true identity as long as you keep consuming stuff. It's no coincidence that most of the people in family businesses whom I have met who have been corrupted by the family's wealth are still consuming beyond their means.

The consumption of stuff doesn't work as a path to fulfillment. Remember: Things don't make you happy. Consuming things to make you happy is like trying to satisfy your hunger for food by listening to music. At best it will distract you, but it can never address your real needs. Your material needs can be met with material stuff, but the other needs can't, and your attempts to find "completion by consumption" will leave you lacking.

Even the word *consumer* seems negative to me. It sounds like someone who takes and takes and ultimately takes too much. If the family wealth is just there for you to consume, then there is not much meaning in it for you, your family, or your community, is there? If you are consuming to try to use stuff to fulfill your emotional needs, then even the consumption will leave you empty and frustrated. If the family's wealth is just your own ATM machine, then it may not help even you.

> **KEYWORD:** In this context, a **consumer** of wealth is one who takes more than he gives. A consumer of wealth is focused on using wealth for self-indulgence and often as a way to avoid dealing with personal, family, and career issues. A consumer is driven by self-interest and is apt to leave far less wealth behind than he was given.

Stewardship

The Bonita Bay Group is an environmentally friendly real estate company in Florida and a family business. When talking with my students and members of my board, the current chair of the company, David Lucas, told them that they have to decide whether they want to be consumers or stewards of wealth. Does the wealth and power you have foster in you any sense of obligation to others or just merely a sense of entitlement to consume?

> **KEYWORD:** A **steward** of wealth uses what he owns to benefit other stakeholders, be they family, the community, the environment, or employees. Stewards often leave more wealth than they were given or at least give more away than they take.

I love the word *stewardship* because I think family businesses can best exemplify this idea not only to the business community, but also to the world. Stewardship is the attitude that even if you own 100 percent of something legally, you feel an obligation to consider and try to benefit other stakeholders. It is how the Native Americans viewed the environment and how many agricultural families view the land. These two groups thought not only of other stakeholders, but they also factored in future generations into their decisions. They held land and wealth as stewards for future generations. Likewise, families that own businesses may feel a sense of obligation to their community, their employees, the environment, and even their heirs.

David Lucas has told me his perspective on this concept:

"...in reality you don't own anything; you are a steward of the assets for someone else. In my case, based on my Christian faith, I see God as the ultimate owner of everything, and I am just the steward of what he has entrusted me with here on this earth. It is my responsibility to manage these assets and deploy them where they will do the most good, not just for my enjoyment and consumption. I also believe I will be called to account for my stewardship when I die and face the Lord."

These are powerful and authentic words to live by.

Human Capital

When you spend your wealth or use your power, are you just consuming it or are you investing it in developing yourself or others? In other words, do you see a difference between investing in an MBA versus buying a new sports car? Do you see the difference between using your wealth to support yourself while you work with the Peace Corps or Habitat for Humanity and using it to pay for a long vacation in the Hamptons?

When you use money and power to create opportunities for people to grow, that is investing in the potential of the person, in their human capital. That type of spending is very different than merely indulgent consumption. Using wealth to help people develop and become better people is perhaps the best use of money and power; such spending makes your parents' struggle and toil much more worthwhile. Indulging yourself might be thought of as eating dessert. A little is good, but too much is unhealthy and becomes less enjoyable. One ice cream cone is fun, but are five ice cream cones that much more fun?

Your Wealth and Your Credibility

If you use your wealth and power to avoid growing up, testing your mettle, and facing the legitimate consequences of your behavior, then it will serve only to erode your credibility. Remember that credibility is self-confidence you feel and others perceive. You may be able to fool yourself and keep your self-confidence high, but you won't fool others for very long. If others perceive you as being able to get away with poor behavior, they will lose respect for you. Whether that behavior is asking for incompletes in college courses or not putting forth your best effort into your job in the family business, other people see and remember it. Does such behavior convey your true character to people? If not, then your reputation is in need of repair.

In the last few years, many people I know who are responsible for hiring people as part of their jobs have told me that they hire on character and develop skills. Now they don't mean that you don't need some basic skills (and credentials) for a given job, but what they do mean is that you can more easily develop someone's skills than you can develop someone's character. What do you think such people will find out if they call your last boss?

Handle Wealth and Power Wisely

Follow these tips for dealing with wealth and power:
- Assess whether you are a consumer or steward of wealth.
- If you are a steward of wealth, then be clear about who the stakeholders are that you feel an obligation to.
- Invest in developing human capital and avoid overindulging yourself.
- Don't use your family's wealth or power to avoid the legitimate consequences of your behavior. Avoiding consequences erodes your credibility.

The Three Players Handle Their Wealth and Power

Assume that a friend of the families of each of the three players owns a large business. That firm is coming to campus to interview for internships next summer. The players are all sophomores, so this summer is an ideal time for an internship. The players' parents call to inform their child about this development and then offer to arrange for their child to be first on the interview list. Furthermore, assume that the player does not have a car to get to the interview, and the parents have offered to help out. So how does each of the players handle these two offers?

The Amateur

Although the firm only wants students with a GPA of 3.0 or more, Tony gets to interview first with his 2.0 GPA because of his family connections. He loves the fact that his connections have gotten him this interview. He even thinks that his parents ought to spring for a fancy rental car (like a Corvette) or, better still, a limousine. Because he has met this family friend before, he doesn't even plan on writing a resume. He figures the person already knows him and his family.

On the three-point analysis, Tony fails to look at his emotional resistance to seeing that his family wealth and power may get him the interview, but without his own credibility, any offer for the internship will be for the wrong reasons. He is not taking ownership for his career. As far as his family's expectations are concerned, Tony and his parents are more than willing to use the family wealth and power to help Tony avoid the legitimate consequences of his behavior. In this case, the legitimate consequence of his poor GPA is that he would not qualify for the internship. In terms of Applied Intelligence, the family friend was embarrassed by Tony showing up in the limousine, not having a resume, and being the least qualified candidate in terms of GPA and character.

The Semipro

Selina feels uncomfortable when she talks to her parents about the interview. Her folks had arranged an interview for her older sister once and had embarrassed her. Selina would like a shot at the interview based on her merits, but her dad insists on putting in a good word for her with the head of this company. They reach a compromise on the car, a nice but not overstated rental car.

Selina feels good that she has the required 3.0 GPA and thinks that the Career Services folks on campus have helped her put together a good resume and cover letter. She is the second candidate to be interviewed (must've been her parents call to this guy). Although she fared better than Tony, she still left the interviewer with mixed feelings about her capabilities. She also forgot to bring the required letters of recommendation or to follow up with a thank-you letter.

Selina is dealing with her emotional resistance by not being corrupted by the wealth and power of her family (she saw how it has affected her sister). Her family's expectations of her are changing because she has made progress with setting a boundary with her folks, especially her father. They are beginning to understand that Selina wants to be responsible for her career decisions. She did not get the internship, but she felt like she improved her Applied Intelligence by learning how to prepare for such an interview.

The Professional

Pat is assertive when talking to her parents. She wants her parents to let her to handle the communications with the interviewer. She wants this interview to happen because of her credibility, not as a favor to the family. So she researches the firm, works with Career Services, and obtains two letters of recommendation. (She even found out one of her professors had worked with this firm and so was an ideal person to write the letter.) She even explains how, as a finance and family business student, this internship aligns with her long-term career plans. She decides to pick out a car for herself and goes for something understated.

Pat is one of the two finalists. She has overcome her emotional resistance and won't be seduced into letting her family help her. She realizes that assistance that comes through her family's wealth and power, although well-intended, just enables her to avoid growing up. She has asserted herself with her family and respectfully conveyed that she is going be responsible for her life and her career. She still wants her parents' help and support, but she wants to be her own person. Her Applied Intelligence is very high, and the family friend tells her folks that he was duly impressed with Pat.

Conclusion

Wealth and the power that comes along with it is very much a double-edged sword. It can help you invest in your development, what I call human capital. It can help you cultivate an attitude of stewardship, of giving back to others, including future generations. It can help you by providing the resources and freedom to figure out who you are.

But wealth has its costs and burdens as well. Wealth and its related power, especially when given at a young age, can seduce you into thinking you don't have to undertake the challenges and struggles of the journey of self-discovery. You can avoid testing your mettle and forging your character through the successes and failures that make a meaningful life. You can try to compensate for these shortcomings in your life by consuming, but you will realize that material things won't solve your personal growth challenges.

Allowing yourself to be seduced into not taking ownership for your career and your life will ultimately cost you two things that are priceless: your credibility and your marketability. Because you have to commit to something to have a life that is meaningful, you need to face this challenge and find the strength, courage, and discipline to do the work to figure out who you want to be.

As you confront the challenges in the rest of the book, keep the main points from this chapter in mind:

- Remember that wealth is both a benefit and a burden. Things don't make you happy.
- Decide if you want to be a steward or a consumer of wealth.
- Own that "completion by consumption" doesn't work.
- Decide if you want (or really how you want) to give back to your community and invest in human capital.
- Recognize that wealth and its related power can make it harder for you to earn your credibility and marketability.

PART III

Facing the Challenges as a Young Adult in the Family Business

P art III is about the challenges that you will confront before and during college. Chapter 7 deals with cultivating credibility instead of seeking refuge in entitlement. Entitlement is the enemy of ownership. Entitlement means you don't have to earn something, whereas ownership means you do. What are you entitled to? What do you want to take ownership for in your life?

Following someone else's script—often written by your parents, but sometimes by your friends, relatives, or even a TV show—is just another way to avoid taking ownership for your life. Even if you succeed at performing someone else's script, the success won't really belong to you because it won't be authentic. Chapter 8 looks at the challenge of writing your own script.

Often, when people can't figure out what else to do, they fall into the family business—not because they want to, but because they have not created other options. This situation leads to the fourth challenge: overcoming your emotional resistance to planning. You need to discover what you want and then come up with a strategy to get it. Planning is a large part of the work you need to do in order to achieve success on your terms.

Chapter 10 is a favorite of mine. I attended college while my family owned a business. You know how much time I spent and help I received to decide if, when, how, and why I should join my family business? None. Very few colleges will help you with this decision. I think that is very wrong! How can you find a college that will offer you support while facing these challenges? This chapter helps you assess both how a college can help you *and* how to address these challenges on your own if necessary.

CHAPTER 7

Challenge 3: Earning Credibility Instead of Feeling Entitled

As defined earlier in this book, credibility is self-confidence that is also legitimate in other people's eyes. Entitlement, on the other hand, is the attitude that you deserve to get something without having to work for it. Entitlement and credibility are a little like television and good conversation—it's hard to have both at the same time. Your challenge is to develop your credibility and avoid entitlement.

When you finish this chapter, you will be able to

- Understand what entitlement is, especially as it relates to family business.
- See the risks of adopting an entitlement attitude related to your education and career.
- Appreciate why no one, not even your parents, can give you credibility.

How Entitlement Can Hurt You

Entitlement is something you don't have to earn. As a human being, you are entitled to basic human rights. As a child, you are entitled to your parents' love. However, if you believe you are entitled to a job in your family business and a share of its ownership and the related wealth merely because you are in the family, then you are at risk.

KEYWORD: In this book, **entitlement** is the attitude that you should be given something without having to earn it.

Feeling entitled concerning the family business may make sense to you. After all, your parents own the business, and they can do whatever they want to with it. But just because they can do something does not mean it is wise for them to do it. Entitlement in the family business is a costly and risky attitude to have. The following sections explain how entitlement can hurt you.

The Entitled Athlete

Think of your favorite sports team. What if the owners of that team had an attitude of entitlement? If the owner of the Yankees decides to place his 20-year-old son at second base even though he is a poor player, what do you think would happen? How would the other players, the fans, and the sports writers view him? Wouldn't they accuse her or him of not earning the position, but merely getting it because Dad owned the Yankees? Do you think that that would increase or decrease the respect people in the sport and the business had for the team? The son might start to brag about how he is good enough to play in the majors, but everyone would know he is really an amateur pretending to be a professional.

Think about how you would feel as the son after playing for the Yankees a few years. At first, it might seem kind of cool. After all, your parents are paying you a million dollars per year. However, the team manager hardly ever puts you in, and you want to play more. Some of the players suck up to you because you are the boss's kid. Other players give you a hard time because they had to earn their way to the pros and you didn't, and you think maybe they're right to feel resentful.

How can you tell if your teammates or your coaches are being honest when they praise you or when they criticize you? Are they sucking up? Just being resentful? You know that you did not earn this position on the team. You didn't go to the tryouts and didn't put in your time playing in the minors (which is a lot like the internships my students have to do). Now you are in your twenties, and it seems awkward to say, "Well, it's my parents' company, and they can do whatever they want with it." That comment would make you seem like an immature family member, not a legitimate pro ballplayer.

You are afraid you may get fired, for a number of reasons. You want the manager to push you the way he does the other players. He won't, because he is afraid you will complain to your parents—not as a player, but as their child. He may be a little bit afraid of keeping you on the bench, but because his contract pays him based on how many games he wins, he is willing to make excuses to your folks about why he doesn't put you into the game more often. So far, your folks seem to buy his excuses, but you wonder if maybe they are aware that keeping you on the bench helps the team win.

You often call in and say you can't make it to practice because of a family commitment, even though you know you shouldn't use your family connection in this way. You know other players can't get away with this behavior. Sometimes you even do it because your parents want you to, and you don't want to make them angry. After all, you have gotten used to having three cars and two condos. You can't afford to lose the million-dollar salary and fall back on your C average finance degree. Besides, if it's true that you have this job only because you are in the family, you had better not make Mom and Dad angry, right? Other times you miss practice just because you know you can get away with it. You feel a little guilty, but what the heck, you're entitled; your folks own the team.

A few years back, your friends told you to take this offer. "Man, what a sweet deal," they would say. "You can chill out, not work hard, and get paid big money." Now you're starting to wonder whether those well-intentioned friends were right.

Of course, you're probably not going to be asked to play for the Yankees. But this example shows what can happen in any family business when members of the next generation think they are entitled to a position that they did not earn and do not have to perform to keep. People in the business resent that person, and that resentment can grow to include the entire family. Even other family members can become uncomfortable with the situation. Although the Yankees example makes this pattern more dramatic, the risk is just as real in your family's business. Don't become like this young ballplayer, destined for a life without credibility.

The Entitled Emperor

In the 2000 film *Gladiator*, which won five Academy Awards including Best Picture, a powerful Roman general, Maximus, is beloved by an ailing Caesar. Privately, Caesar selects Maximus as his successor to rule Rome and return power to the people via the senate. Caesar tells Maximus he is the son he should have had.

Later that evening Caesar tells his only son, Commodus, of his succession plan. Commodus is an amateur; in fact, he is so insecure and lacking in credibility that he feels entitled to everything and anything. This ultimate amateur murders his own father. His lack of credibility and selfishness result in his overthrow by his own sister, the Roman senate, and Maximus, who unite to overcome this leader who came to power for all the wrong reasons. (The movie has some great fight scenes, too!)

An Unearned Opportunity

I often see sons and daughters in family business who have been given jobs they didn't earn, and I have never seen one of them who is happy. Mark Hollis is a leader of Publix Supermarkets, one of the largest family businesses in the United States. In his visits to campus to talk with my students, Hollis has said, "You gotta wanna." You have to want to succeed, and in order to truly succeed, you have to earn your position on the team.

It's very sad to encounter a young person who believes he or she is a professional when everyone around him or her believes otherwise. No matter how silver the platter, you can't be handed *credibility*. You have to earn it.

> **KEYWORD:** Credibility is having self-confidence (the internal part) and having others perceive that confidence as legitimate (the external part).

I worked with one member of the next generation who was hired directly out of college. The father felt like he could work with his son on a lot of his problems: an attitude of entitlement, a resistance to hard work, and very little outside experience. His father mentioned behavior that would have probably resulted in any other employee's termination, such as his son bragging that he could get away with running personal expenses through the company expense account because the bookkeeper was afraid to confront him. I imagine others in the business, and probably the rest of the family, think the son had failed to legitimately earn his position and perform at a level that warranted him keeping his job. His parents eventually decided they needed, for everyone's sake, to let him go. That's not where you want to end up, is it?

Find Your Own Motivation

Worth magazine goes to 100,000 readers each month whose net worth averages over $5 million. For the April 2006 issue (which also featured a nice article about the Stetson Family Business Program), I was asked to respond to a reader's question that is typical of many asked by family business parents:

Continued

Continued

"My son is in his final year of college, and we are in a struggle over his next move. I would like to see him take a job in the business world, either with our family company or some other firm. He wants to study philosophy at the graduate level. His argument is that we have plenty of money, and he really does not need to worry about earning a wage. In purely economic terms, he is right. But I built the company that created our wealth, and I know how important it was in terms of character building to have taken on that huge challenge. How do I convince him not to take the easy way out?"

You can see Mom or Dad is concerned that the son's sense of entitlement will erode his credibility, which they call character. I wrote that the parents should discuss with their son his motivation for going to graduate school. Does he have a passion for philosophy? Is he motivated by a desire to give back to the world? Or is this simply a way for him avoid growing up, avoid testing his mettle, and avoid finding out who he really is by misusing the family wealth. What would you tell the parents in this situation? The son?

What Your Credibility Means to the Family Business

Would you invest your life savings and your family's future in something that had a 70 percent chance of failing? That is exactly what you are doing if you decide to join your family business. Out of every 100 family businesses started, only 33 or so are still owned by the family in the second generation. The failure most often occurs when the family tries to transfer control from the first generation to the second. Of the family businesses that do make it successfully to the second generation, only 30 percent of those successfully transition to the third generation. This means that if you are a second-generation family business owner, there's only one chance in nine that you will pass your family's business on to your children. Now that you know those are the odds, don't you want to do everything you can to increase your chances of financial success and family well-being?

Family businesses tend to fail for two main reasons: lack of planning, which includes setting the strategic direction for the business, and lack of preparing for the transfer between generations, which includes developing the leadership of the next generation. Thus planning and preparing for the generational transfer are the two most important things you can do.

The best way that you as an individual can prepare for such a transfer is to build your credibility. A key step in this effort is to develop a personal life plan, a process that is described in Chapter 13. If you have an attitude of entitlement, you may well feel you don't need to work on your credibility. But if you have not earned both credibility and marketability before you start talking about succession, chances are good that your family business will end up in that 70 percent of family businesses that fail.

In many family businesses, everyone feels as if they are waiting for the rest of the family to make a decision. I challenge you to start working on yourself and not wait for anyone else. You have to figure out who you are and where you want to go. Taking ownership for your future is not only a great way to model your own response-ability, which enhances your credibility, but it also puts positive pressure on your family to start planning, too. It seems strange, but you are far more likely to bring about healthy change in your family if you consider changing your own behavior.

Decide Whether to Work in the Family Business

When choosing whether to work for your family's business, consider the following:

- Work with your family business only if you have the self-discipline needed to earn credibility.
- Work with your family business only if your family shares your attitude about the importance of credibility.
- Gaining outside experience almost always adds to both your internal and external sense of credibility.
- Having outside experience helps you see where you feel entitled in your family's business and gives you empathy for the nonfamily employees.

The Three Players Try to Earn Credibility

Let's look at how the three players deal with the challenge of earning credibility and avoiding entitlement. Each player will by evaluated according to the three-point analysis of emotional resistance, family expectations, and Applied Intelligence.

The Amateur

Because his mom owns 100 percent of a law firm, Tony thinks he has a job waiting for him. Tony blows off classes, never develops a resume, never does an internship outside of his own family business, and always underperforms. He has selected general business mostly because it seems easy and he can't figure out what else to do. He tells people he is a pre-law student, even though his school has no such major. "What difference does it make?" he says. "I have a job regardless of my grades.

Tony has 2.0 grade point average, which is a C average. With these grades, chances are next to nil that he can get into a law school, yet he has convinced himself that he still deserves a job in the family law firm. Even the other professionals in the firm who aren't lawyers have college degrees and at least a B average. Perhaps without realizing it, he has set himself up to be a charity case who the family business may hire only because no one else will have him. His coworkers, however, will not grant him any credibility he hasn't earned.

Also, if Tony were honest with himself, he would tell you he is kind of intimidated by the thought of someone at another company being his boss. What if that person told him he was no good? What if that person confronted him on his grades, his lack of experience, or his tendency to always be late?

Tony has not dealt with his emotional resistance relating to his fear of failure, which keeps him from trying to work anywhere else. He has not dealt with his family's expectations about his joining the family business. He has an attitude of entitlement, which his family may share. Finally, he has not looked at the massive Applied Intelligence risk of being viewed as the charity case and hired by his family for all the wrong reasons. His attitude of entitlement also prevents him from earning credibility. Tony is an amateur and has done a poor job with this challenge.

The Semipro

Selina, the semipro, goes to school and works hard, but she never steps back and addresses what she really wants to do. She realizes that college is like a new career that requires not only new skills, but also a new perspective. It feels different from high school, where her teachers and parents were always watching over her, giving steady reminders, and compensating for her shortcomings. Selina is now trying to be responsible for her success or failure in college, but she is confused and frustrated. She does not know if she really likes her major; she picked it because a friend of the family works in that field, and "it kind of sounded interesting." As an accounting major, she is looking at careers in the field of accounting outside her family business.

Her dad promised her a great salary that is $20,000 higher than other kids in her graduating class are getting. Yet she knows she got that offer because she is his daughter, not because she has earned it through her skills, credentials, or experiences. Although Selina may not have an attitude of entitlement, her father seems to encourage her to develop one. She is making progress on this topic with her dad, but it has been slow.

Although she isn't sure that she wants to work in accounting, she is probably going to take an accounting position with another company, if only to avoid being trapped working for the family business. She had seen how unhappy her older sister has been there for the last few years. It seems as though either way she turns, she is not going to be happy.

Semipros like Selina often have the best of intentions, but they are missing some element that enables them to perform at the professional level. Maybe they don't take complete ownership for their life, or maybe they lack motivation or self-discipline. Just like professional athletes have to push themselves to train, study, and to constantly get feedback on their performance, you have to expect to do the same if you want to play at that level.

Selina has started to deal with her emotional resistance about what she wants to do with her education and career. She needs some help and more work, but she is aware of her fear of taking the easy way out and repeating her sister's mistake. She needs to discuss some issues with her family, such as why her sister is working there when she is miserable. And why is her father willing to overpay Selena, which is a setup for eroding her credibility? Selena may need to realize that her family has the attitude that family members are entitled to be hired and overpaid.

On the Applied Intelligence front, Selina has the courage not to take the easy way out. She deserves credit for trying to be a self-made person. However, she shouldn't pursue a career she may not like just to avoid the family business, so she still needs to do the work to align her personality, values, and skills with a career.

The Professional

Pat is committed to finding her own path. She began by paying attention to some of the self-assessment tools that teachers have used in high school and college, like the Myers-Briggs Type Indicator (MBTI). (Chapter 13 explains what the MBTI is and how it can be used.) In addition to talking with people at the Career Center and her faculty advisor, she also has her favorite aunt acting as a career mentor. This aunt not only knows her family business, but also has a career as a chief financial officer at a large local company. The process of choosing a career path has been a struggle, but she is learning who she is and what she wants.

Pat has decided on a dual major in family business and finance, which is in sync with her personality type. She has even shadowed her aunt at work for a few days and talked to her about career possibilities. Pat is making progress toward getting an internship with a family business this summer to see if she will like it. To that end, she not only has created a resume, but also has worked for a couple of hours with her faculty advisor, a finance professor, to plan out the remaining five semesters of courses to take. She has shown this plan to her aunt and is starting to think more about what she wants on her resume when she graduates in order to land that finance job she wants. Pat's a professional, so she has reflected on who she is and what she wants out of a career, and she is talking with her aunt and her advisor about the requirements for the career she wants.

Pat's parents own and operate a company that owns hotels in three states. Originally, her folks thought she was entitled to a job in sales or marketing. Over the last few years, as Pat has taken greater ownership for her life, her folks have stopped telling Pat, "You can always work here. It will be a little easier for you." That isn't what Pat wants, and now it is not what her parents want for her, either.

Pat and her folks have agreed that a few years of working with another company outside the family business is a good way for her to develop the skills, credentials, and experiences that will add a lot to the family business. She wants people to respect her because of her business abilities, not because of her family connections. Pat's parents also see why she could contribute more in a finance position than in the sales position they had originally thought up for her. All this has evolved as Pat worked on herself, discussed plans with her family, and as everyone took time to reflect.

Pat has done very well on the three-point analysis. She has dealt with her emotional resistance by figuring out who she is and what that means for her education and career. She has set some boundaries with her family, has had some good discussions, and is managing the family business opportunity. In terms of her Applied Intelligence, she is conveying her character to others. She is responsibly following a career that interests her, and in the process, she is getting support, feedback, and advice from her mentor and faculty advisor.

Why You Need to Take Ownership of Your Credibility

Think about what your parents owning a business means to you. To what does it entitle you? Before you can begin to consider taking a job with the family business, you need to know what being a member of the family entitles you to in relation to the family business.

Discuss the following questions with your family:

- Are you entitled to consideration for a job in the family business as long as you are qualified?
- Provided that you perform well, are you entitled to keep your job in the family business?

Most people would answer yes to these questions because they agree that these entitlements are fair. You can still build your credibility if you get and keep a job in the family business under these conditions.

If you have decided to work in the family business, ask yourself and the members of your family the following questions:

- Do you have the same or better qualifications as the nonfamily employees in the business?
- Are you held to the same level of performance expectations in your job as the other employees?
- Is your salary the same as other employees who are doing the same work?

An answer of no to these questions erodes your credibility. This kind of entitlement is destructive to you, your family, and the business.

If you lack the self-discipline to work hard in your family's business, then start in a different job where you won't feel entitled to anything your performance hasn't earned you. You will then have the positive pressure to show up, work hard, and prove yourself, and that's how you earn credibility.

Nobody wants to be a victim. Still, people often complain, "If only someone in my family would change, then I would be happy. If only my dad wouldn't criticize me so much! If only my sister wouldn't compete so much with me! If only my mom wouldn't treat me like a kid!" Think of the "if only" statements you make related to your family. They might come true. Your family might change, and you can certainly ask, hope, and pray for them to change. However, if you make your happiness dependent on that, you are giving away your power to control your own life. Taking ownership starts with deciding what do you need to do even if no one else changes. Making this decision is a big part of what distinguishes an amateur from a professional.

If you develop your sense of ownership, you can no longer believe in entitlement. Why? Because entitlement means that someone else is responsible for your life and future. Success starts with you, today, taking ownership for your future.

Conclusion

If you believe that being a family member gives you free ownership or a guaranteed position in the family business, you risk eroding your credibility. With that attitude, you are no longer motivated to develop your credibility. You might be hired or retained only because of your last name, for example, but eventually the employees, the family, and even you will realize that. You will be sadly lacking in credibility and probably will not be marketable.

Entitlement robs you of the opportunity to pursuing your own path, finding your passion, and becoming your own person. You have to decide if at graduation you want to earn the right to feel credible and be viewed by other businesses in the marketplace as marketable. Are you willing to accept that you are responsible for your actions, for your responses to whatever life throws at you, for your future, and for your happiness? That is what ownership means. Of course, you still want people to help you, to be supportive, and to give you advice. However, no one is ever going to care as much about your life as you.

Remember these tips for earning credibility and avoiding entitlement:

- Cultivate an attitude of ownership. Your life and your success are your responsibility.

Continued

Continued

- You can't succeed if you can't really fail, so you need to test yourself.
- If your family business seems like the easy way out, then don't take it, because it isn't.
- You need to be able to talk with your parents as an adult, and vice versa.
- Develop healthy boundaries between your life, your family, and the family business.
- Remember that entitlement is the enemy of credibility.

CHAPTER 8

Challenge 4: Writing Your Own Script

A student told me about her father, a hard-driving entrepreneur who had founded the family business. Her father offered her a generous salary to work for him. As a college senior, she had received a job offer from at least one other company and was both very credible and marketable, yet she felt both emotional and financial pressure to join her father's business. She gave the impression that if it had not been for her father's dramatic, last-minute offer "she couldn't refuse," she would have started her career outside the family business. It seemed to me that working for the family business was not what she wanted for herself, but it was what her dad wanted for her.

If success means becoming your own person and living according to your values, then simply following your parents' plans for you ain't success. This chapter will help you be able to

- Realize the challenge created by having successful, powerful, and persuasive people set a course for your future.
- Take ownership for your part in this pattern.
- Realize why you need to do the work to meet this challenge.

Resisting Others' Scripts for You

A phrase I use to describe people who take ownership for their lives, do the necessary self-reflection, and live in accordance with their values is *writing their own script*. By that I mean that they are not merely like actors in a movie who are playing a part that someone else, be it their parents, their spouse, their friends, or a group they are a member of, wrote for them. They are living an authentic life of their own making.

> **KEYWORD:** Writing your own script means doing the necessary self-reflection and values clarification in order to live a life that is truly your own.

If you don't take the time to figure out what is important to you, a view of your future set out by your parents, friends, or teachers may sound better than anything you could formulate on your own. Any college student can easily fall into this trap. However, if your parents are strong, successful people who run a business, they are probably pretty good at persuading others, especially their children, to their point of view. Even if you have a vision of your future, your business-owning parents are likely to be so powerful, persuasive, and confident that their opinion can easily overwhelm you.

Chapter 9 explains how to figure out what you want to do. In this chapter, the focus is on navigating through your relationship with your parents and taking ownership for your future. Taking ownership means that even if your parents are not overwhelming, but just well-intended, they cannot write your script. (That goes for teachers and friends, too.)

If you're following someone else's script, your success will never be an authentic success. Not only will you end up in a career you did not select, but also you will have failed to develop the confidence and overall credibility to make career decisions for yourself.

Don't Be a Mini-Me

In the 1999 movie **Austin Powers: The Spy Who Shagged** Me (a sequel to the 1997 film **Austin Powers: International Man of Mystery**, supervillian Dr. Evil, disappointed that his son Scott has no desire to someday run the family business, is delighted to discover that his colleagues at work have cloned Mini-Me, a smaller scale version of himself. Mini-Me is a great metaphor for that tendency most parents have: To one degree or another, they want their kids to be like them, to be younger versions of themselves, and to grow up and fulfill the parents' destiny. Are you destined to be a Mini-Me or your own person?

The Power of Parents

Your parents care about you a great deal, are transitioning away from being your decision maker (just as you are individuating—funny how that all works, huh?), and probably have a lot of your respect, at least on career issues. Allowing your parents to write your script is an easy challenge to succumb to. I know, because early on in my career I made the mistake of following my parents' script for me.

My parents weren't overwhelming, but they were persuasive. I started out in public accounting, which is a great career for many people, but was wrong for me. My father had started out in accounting and had shifted into entrepreneurship. He felt that all business boiled down to numbers and people, and it is better to learn the numbers in school and the people on the job than vice versa. Also, back in the late 80s (that's 1980s, not 1880s), accounting was one of the top-paying careers. It all sounded logical and satisfying. Without a firm sense of who I was and what I wanted to do, their script looked a lot better than mine.

My career suffered because I didn't do the hard self-reflection and figure out who I was, what I wanted, and what career would be best for me. I waited until I was 30 to buckle down and do the work necessary to move from being a semipro to a professional. I want to save you from the decade-long struggle that I went through.

Many of my students face this same risk. Their parents are worried about their future and offer some good advice, but the students haven't made the necessary shifts in attitude or done the work necessary to come up with their own career path. If the student follows a path chosen for them by their parents, the path never feels quite right. They always end up wondering if they're on the right track. Over time, these doubts will linger and grow.

Your Career Choice

Within four years of graduation, many people will not be working in the field in which they majored in college, according to the U.S. Department of Education. Why is this? I think the reason is that students do not take the time to think about who they are and choose a major and career that fits them.

I see people of all ages who don't so much choose a career as end up in one. When you ask them why they selected a certain career path, they rattle off a list of reasons that don't sound very real and that don't convince anyone (not even themselves) that they put much thought into their career choice. For example, I hear people say they decided to teach for the summers off. To be sure, that's a great perk. However, really dedicated teachers are too underpaid and teaching is too draining (between the students and the administration, you could drain the life out of a saint) to do it just for summers off. I usually think such people are reading off of someone else's script, and I understand that firsthand. Before I wrote my own script at age 30, I would have rattled off a list of all the reasons my dad gave for why I should pick public accounting.

If you are ungrounded in your goals, you become like a sailboat without a rudder. You move in whatever direction the wind blows. That wind can come from your parents or other people. For example, it can come from a great class or teacher. I have always been concerned about students who suddenly want to go to law school merely because they liked having me as their teacher for one business law course. A wise friend or relative also may push you in a certain direction. Although listening to these people and taking their advice into consideration is acceptable, you shouldn't let them make the decision for you. You benefit greatly from going through the process of figuring out what you want and deciding for yourself. That struggle makes the decision far more meaningful and one that you can really own.

Find the Career That Fits You

When you contemplate your career choices, keep these tips in mind:
- If you think your family business is the easy way out, you are completely wrong.
- If someone else's advice sounds better than your career plan, you need to develop a better career plan.
- If you aren't clear on who you are and what you value, you are unlikely to find a career that is you and that you value.
- If you don't figure out who you are, what you value, and where you want to go, you will never develop credibility.

Following the Family Business Script

You are at risk because your family's business can make it too easy to not work on your own script. You've probably already worked in the family business, and it seems like a safe place, a known quantity. You can be easily seduced into thinking, "Well, working for my family business makes sense." You can tell yourself, "Now I don't have to address that gigantic decision about what to do with my life. I sort of tried, and nothing really clicked."

As business owners, your parents are probably more persuasive than the average parent. Beyond that, they can actually offer you the career they think you should follow. They also think the world of you and see all your potential. They understand and accept you, and they look beyond traits like being late, overly quiet, disorganized, or otherwise in need of development. Another boss may be less tolerant of the same traits.

Many of my students think going into the family business is easier than working elsewhere. They think they won't have to work as hard, and they won't have to spend time figuring out what to do with their lives. Ultimately, however, working for the family business is neither easy nor simple.

At the same time, many parents tell me they are concerned, if not downright frightened, at the prospect of their children entering the family business. They know running your own business can be hard and can put a heck of a lot pressure on you. That pressure is even worse if you don't have your heart in the business.

I remember a student who came to see me to say she was going back into the family business. When I asked her why, she answered, "It is my turn to suffer." Wow! That was a shocker! Fortunately, she decided not to go back to that career. I hope you won't, either, not for a script like that.

Breaking Under Parental Pressure

The story of Henry Ford and his only son, Edsel, seems to epitomize the negative consequences of letting parents write the script for their children. Henry Ford founded the Ford Motor Company, which is to this day a family business. By all accounts, he was a demanding boss and father.

In the 1986 **New York Times** article, "Intrigue and Tyranny in Motor City," Ted Morgan wrote that Edsel was "expected to succeed the father." But the article goes on to say that Henry plotted against his son, constantly humiliating him and keeping him an "underling," thus destroying his credibility. Even though Edsel was president of Ford, Henry backed Harry Bennett in every dispute between Edsel and Harry.

Many people attribute Edsel's ulcers and other health issues and even his early death at age 49 to the stress of working under his controlling and manipulative father. It is hard to imagine that this outcome was the script Edsel wanted for his life.

Starting Your Own Script

I am amazed that people invest years and tens of thousands of dollars on college and graduate school to train for a career, but they put almost no time or resources into figuring out what career they want. It seems a little out of whack, doesn't it?

The professional realizes that much of this work is personal. It takes individuation, clarifying who you are. At the same time, it requires clarifying your values (not adopting your friends', family's, or coworkers' values) and crafting a vision of success. It takes working with the emotional resistance in your life. Finally, it requires you to realize that the time to grow up and take ownership for your life is now, not next year, not after you graduate, and certainly not after you join the family business.

Perhaps you are feeling motivated to get to work. Maybe you're even jumping up and down for the chance to get started at this point, (Hey, I can dream, can't I?) or at least engaged enough to keep reading and ask, "Okay, how do I begin?"

Self-Reflection

Writing your own script means doing some honest self-reflection and self-assessment. That means taking a hard look at your strengths and areas you need to improve, and owning them. Consider the following questions as you think about taking ownership for your future:

- Who is responsible for your career and your future?
- What is your family's attitude toward you and your future?
- How does your parents' view of your future influence you?
- How does your parents' view of your future relate to your role in the family?
- What are the costs and benefits of your parent's view of your future to you? What are the costs and benefits to the family?
- Does your career choice affect whether you receive any of the family wealth or ownership in the family business?
- How do you best prepare to talk with your family?

- What might be a good time to begin discussing your future with your family?
- What are three to five concrete behaviors your parents could see that would make you more credible (personally and professionally) in their eyes in the next two to four years?
- What do you need to do if your family never changes?

Consider discussing your answers to these questions with a friend or insightful family member.

Emotional Resistance

I think there is more emotional resistance around selecting a career than just about anything else. You may feel unprepared to make such a gigantic decision, or you may be afraid that if you mess up this choice, you may devastate your life. Suppose you have chosen to be a marketing major, but after taking one course in that major, you decide you don't like it. If you are like most students, you will say, "Well, I have to major in marketing, or else I will fall behind." The logic is that because you have already taken a course, you are trapped in this career path.

Under these stressful circumstances, having someone you respect give you a career path and the reasons to follow it may seem quick and efficient. In this way, following someone else's script may seem to serve you. But look at the costs of following someone else's script, and decide if that is what you really want. What are the chances you will be happy in a career someone else selects for you? Do they know your personality as well as you do or should? Do they know and understand your core values? Do you? Do they know your personal definition of success? Do you?

Ownership

I once had a student who said he was going to be a doctor. In less than an hour, with the other students asking him some pretty obvious questions, such as, "Do you have the grades to get into medical school?" he was shocked to admit that he really didn't want to be a doctor and couldn't get into medical school even if he wanted to. He also admitted that being a doctor was his parents' script, and he desperately did not want to disappoint them. In that session, my student had a huge shift in awareness. He walked around shell-shocked for a few days before he realized he needed to do some work and take ownership for his life.

Have you picked a major and a career path based upon a realistic assessment of yourself and of what the career involves? Part of success is authenticity, which is doing what works for you. You can seek out others' advice, but if you don't make decisions that feel right for you, you greatly diminish your chances of being happy. That is why letting other people tell you what to do doesn't work. They almost never base their opinions on an assessment and understanding of how you would define success. And how could they, if even you haven't done this yet?

For you be able to meet this challenge, you must realize that having an attitude of ownership is the best way to avoid merely following someone else's script. You have to come up with your own script. If you have no vision for your future, anyone else's vision will look better than yours, won't it? It is pretty easy to lose a race if you haven't entered your horse in it.

As you begin to make the attitude shift towards ownership, watch how your interaction with your family changes. Maybe you call your parents less often for solutions to your problems and more often for advice on how you plan to solve them. Maybe you start going to other people, like professors, for advice, going to friends for support, and going to Career Services on campus for feedback instead of going to your folks all the time. Maybe you become more proactive and less reactive. Are you now more likely to talk with them about an internship you want to do in a year than you are to call in a panic about your car being towed yesterday because of $350 in unpaid parking tickets? I hope so.

The Three Players Face Their Parents' Script

This chapter is about writing your own script and not letting your parents or anyone else determine your future. The following sections describe how the three players try to establish their own identities instead of defaulting to their parents' script.

The Amateur

Tony is looking for the easiest script and does not even think about writing one of his own. Because of this, he is more at risk for accepting his parents' script or any other script that looks good. This lack of ownership often prompts him to blame others when things don't work out. He doesn't seem to realize that not deciding for yourself really is deciding. It is deciding to set yourself up for failure.

Tony still thinks his parents' idea that he will go to law school and become a partner in the firm right after graduating makes a lot of sense. He says, "I really want to be a lawyer." However, he has invested no time in that goal, and he has a 2.0 GPA. During a peer feedback session, Tony's script did not hold up well under questioning.

In the three-point analysis, Tony's biggest issue is his own emotional resistance to stepping up to the plate and deciding what he wants out of his life. He needs to decide who he wants to be when he grows up. Hopefully, he will eventually do so, but I have dealt with people in their 70s who haven't gotten around to it yet. In the meantime, he has accepted his parents' script and avoided writing his own. This decision will never lead to authentic success because it is not based on what he wants.

On the Applied Intelligence front, others will inevitably see Tony as someone who did not have the character to do the work necessary to establish his own identity separate from his family, which you need to do even if you choose to work in the family business. Because of that fundamental issue, Tony has not talked with his folks about letting him set his own career or life course. Tony's character is compromised by this reluctance to face making an authentic career choice, and people see that he is not his own person. As he gets older and more entrenched in not taking ownership for his life and career, his emotional resistance will increase. Don't follow Tony's example.

The Semipro

Selina either isn't sure how to choose a career or has trouble getting around to doing it. She is only a sophomore, but her parents have already told her she can work in the family business and manage one of their restaurants. She knows some of the people at the restaurant and thinks they're nice, but she doesn't think she would enjoy management. Also, this job doesn't align with her major in accounting. Her older sister, Christina, started working there two years ago, and it doesn't seem to be working out. Her parents demand a lot from Christina, and they fight over things like the hours she works, the vacation days she takes, and the benefits she is due.

Selina is very tentative about discussing her thoughts about a career with her parents and making it clear that she will be the one to take responsibility for her future. Sometimes the path her parents suggest seems like the path of least resistance. She is unsure and is struggling with the decision. However, she has reached out to some people she trusts for advice and has started the process of self-reflection. She has even attended some career services events.

Selina is making progress on her emotional resistance, some progress on the boundaries with her family, and significant progress on her Applied Intelligence. She has at least started the journey.

The Professional

Pat entered college with a commitment to write her own script. The first family business course she took helped her understand that the other students whose families owned businesses were going through similar struggles. Like most college students, each was managing a changing relationship with their parents. The family business students, however, were all going through those changes in the context of the three potentially lifelong relationships: family, employee, and owner/heir. Talking with the others in the group helped her examine and start to deal with her own emotional resistance.

Pat has begun an ongoing dialogue with her parents about what she wants and what they want for her. Her dad was pretty resistant at first, thinking that Pat was too young to know what is best for her future. Pat appreciated having the family business course that allowed her to talk with both her peers and her professors about how to handle this situation. It helped her to hear how other students, especially the girls in the program, were dealing with their fathers.

As her parents have seen Pat commit to doing the work, she has gained credibility in their eyes. They see she is willing to seek out resources, look for a mentor, talk with her professors, and generally take responsibility for her future.

On the three-point analysis, Pat has started to confront her emotional resistance. She sees the discussion with her family as a long-term process, not a one-time event. Her peers, professors, and parents see her as willing to take ownership for her future. She seeks advice, support and feedback, but she still makes her own decisions. Her Applied Intelligence is very strong, and her reputation reflects her willingness to be proactive, responsible, and self-aware.

Conclusion

This chapter is about the influence you give others over your life and what you want to do with that pattern. Once you become aware of this pattern, you can decide to take ownership for your part in it. This is when you begin to take ownership for your future.

Realize the risk of having successful, powerful, and persuasive people set your future. Your parents are most likely powerful, persuasive people whom you trust and admire. Although they want what is best for you and they can give you their opinion, do not accept this opinion as a substitute for your choice. Your parents, friends, and other advisors can be helpful, but they should not make decisions for you.

This life stage is about shifting toward having your own opinions and decisions, and then accepting responsibility for them. Whatever path you decide to follow, make certain that it is really yours. If it is not really your decision, you fail by not learning to make your own decisions and by not selecting an authentic path to success. To become credible, you have to have the self-confidence to make your own decisions, even if they don't always agree with other people's opinions. You have to write your own script.

Keep these thoughts in mind:

- Your parents are going to offer advice because they care, but you have to make your own choices.
- It is your job to find your own path.
- Asking for help in the form of feedback, support, and advice is a good idea.
- Keep the dialogue open and honest with your family about expectations and plans for your future.
- Having the courage and skill to assess a career path is perhaps even more important than which path you select.

Challenge 5: Planning Your Career

After more than 16 years as a college professor, I am amazed by how little time and consideration people invest in selecting their careers. They pour staggering amounts of time and money into their education to work on the path they have chosen, but they won't step back and do the work necessary to ensure they have chosen the right path. Curious, isn't it?

I have seen many of my students pick a career path based on poor reasoning. They have been overly influenced by their parents, a professor, a TV show, a relative, or friends. Sadly, they have wasted their time, a lot of money, and expended at least some of their potential on ineffective attempts to find a fulfilling career.

This chapter shows you that in order to find a satisfying career, you first have to know what you want and then you have to make a plan to get it. By the end of this chapter, you will be able to

- Take advantage of your time in college to figure out which career best suits your personality and begin to prepare for it.
- Overcome your emotional resistance to career planning.
- Manage your career throughout your lifetime by using your career planning skills.

College and Career Planning

I don't think colleges do a good job at helping students choose their careers. Although there are wonderful exceptions, including the people who run career services departments on many campuses, I think the problem is too complex for the short shrift it receives at many colleges.

First, I think many students have an attitude problem about this issue. They think if they get good grades, then the college is responsible for helping them find a rewarding career. Colleges can help with a career search, but they can't make this decision for you. In my experience, colleges are better at helping you follow a path once you have selected it than helping you to find the right path.

In my opinion, colleges would serve students better by *intervening* on that attitude. Beginning your first day on campus, colleges should help you realize that you, not the college and not your parents, are the one primarily responsible for determining your future.

> **KEYWORD:** Intervening is a type of feedback in which you help another person see the harmful consequences of continuing the same pattern of behavior. You use it with the hope the other person will be able to make better choices in the future. For example, a person's inappropriate drinking on the job would warrant an intervening discussion.

Another attitude problem is students from family businesses who think college itself is a waste of time because they already know that they have jobs in the family business. (This attitude is explored in Chapter 10.) Until colleges work to change their students' attitudes or shift their awareness, those students will be stuck in a mindset that will not cultivate their credibility.

The positive pressure that students from families without family businesses feel can help them to step up to the challenge of choosing and planning for a career because they are more apt to realize that what happens after graduation is dependent upon them. If your family owns a business, you will probably need to have even greater maturity and self-discipline to deal with this challenge instead of avoiding it.

College is a good time to start to take ownership for your life, your career, and your own happiness. I have never heard anyone who has graduated agree that figuring all this out after graduation is easier. So while you have four years to take advantage of the courses, the professors, Career Services department, and all the other resources, start writing your own script. The important thing is to realize that family, friends, and college can help, but no one else will ever be able to write an authentic script for your life.

Start Your Script Now

Keep these dos and don'ts in mind when you start to write your life plan in college:

- Don't think starting as a freshman is too early.
- Don't think starting as a senior is too late.
- Don't kid yourself that it is easier to start this work after graduation.
- Do compare how much effort you invest in getting your major with how much effort you are willing to invest to manage your life.
- Do have a clear understanding of your personality, your values, and your own definition of success.
- Do consider getting a mentor who is neither family nor friend.

Hard Work, Great Rewards

From what I've seen, and some reported studies seem to bear this out, very few people ever sit down and draft a life plan. One reason is that it's hard. Making a life plan and choosing the right career brings up that old issue of emotional resistance.

For almost 15 years, I had a standing offer with my students, friends, family, and peers that I would buy lunch or dinner for anyone who worked all the exercises in Richard Nelson Bolles's book *What Color Is Your Parachute?* I have probably made that offer to almost 2,000 people now, and I have had to buy exactly two meals. The book is a classic, and it works. (I know, because I used it.) It has sold millions and millions of copies. Yet based on my experience, few people work the exercises in it. Why? Because it is a difficult process. However, that is where the value is. Would you buy a book on exercise and expect to get in shape by reading it but without ever doing any of the exercises?

To overcome some of that emotional resistance to planning a career, consider these facts. The latest statistics indicate that people in college today may have more than three careers and seven jobs in their lifetimes. (These statistics are found in Michelle Casto's book *Get Smart! About Modern Career Development: A Personal Guide to Creating Your Life's Work.*) Add to that the statistic from the Department of Education that by four years after graduation, about half of college graduates do not work in the field in which they majored. So what does all that mean? It means the ability to effectively manage your career is much more important today than it used to be. That is why you need to clarify to yourself who you are and what you value.

Time invested in the necessary tasks to choose a career will reap major rewards because you will have a career that suits who you are. Thoughtful career planning works, as illustrated in the examples in the following sections.

Follow Your Values to Find Your Path

In the 1994 movie **Little Big League**, the owner of the Minnesota Twins professional baseball team dies, leaving ownership of the team to his 12-year-old grandson, Billy (somewhat like the Yankees example I used in Chapter 7). In the movie, the grandson is a baseball wiz kid and goes a long way toward proving himself credible to the team, the sportswriters, the fans, and even himself.

However, Billy decides that even though he can do it, owning and operating a baseball team is not the right path for a 12-year-old. He wants to be a kid and hang out with his friends and play ball in the street instead. Even though other people see him as being successful, his work doesn't align with his values. Ultimately, he finds and follows his authentic path.

Planning for Success

I often tell people that I had the career part of my mid-life crisis early. By the time I was 30, I had already gone from public accounting to my family's health care business, then to law school, and finally to an entrepreneurial family business where I worked with my dad and younger brother. I was feeling dissatisfied. I was tired of switching careers and moving, proving myself, and hoping that I would like the results.

During the year surrounding my thirtieth birthday, I did three things that led me to my teaching career, which I love. First, I worked every exercise in *What Color Is Your Parachute?* It took a lot of energy to overcome my own emotional resistance to that task. Second, I asked people I knew if they liked their jobs, and I was astonished to learn that most people were basically dissatisfied. Third, I set a primary goal to create a career where I would look forward to getting up and going to work each morning.

During all this self-assessment and planning, I came up with 13 goals. One year later, I was achieving 11 of them. After two years, I was achieving number 12, and number 13 was coming along. That's not a bad track record, is it? I refused to believe that I could not be happy with my career, refused to believe happiness and success were a function of luck, and refused to believe I was a victim of circumstance.

Perhaps you're thinking, "Well, that's all right for you. But you're a smart guy with a graduate degree. That wouldn't work for an ordinary Joe (or Jo) like me." In the next section, you can read about a student of mine who has taken the same steps I did and found his own version of success.

Getting What You Really Want

Students often come into my office and talk with me about their career plans. They pause and look around, as if to make sure no one is listening in, and then they say to me, "You know what I really want to do?" Of course, I usually don't know until they tell me.

Mark Maundrell, a management major who thought he was supposed to become a manager, leaned in and confided, "I really want to be a professional golfer." My response might surprise you. Instead of telling him that was a silly idea (or advising him to follow his bliss), I asked, "Would you be willing to invest 20 to 40 hours in assessing a career in which you might truly want to spend the next 50 years of your life?"

Mark was a great athlete in high school, but when he got into college, he felt somewhat lost and not fully motivated. When he was a sophomore going through the very first family business course, Mark latched onto the idea of planning and invested over 40 hours in creating a life plan related to pursuing a career as a professional golfer.

During that semester, I had dinner with Mark and his parents. His father was a successful lawyer who was also very interested in sports. He coached a sports team and had always been supportive of Mark. He liked the idea of Mark becoming a professional golfer, but he was concerned about whether Mark was really serious about it. Like most people at age 19, Mark had some credibility issues with his dad. Mark proved that he was serious by planning his work, and then working his plan. This young man not only lined up an internship at the Golf Channel and came up with a budget and training schedule to show his dad, but he also researched what a career as a golf professional was really like.

The odds for any given golfer to make it as a professional are not that great. Mark realized this, and he still wanted to give it a shot. At his core, Mark felt he would succeed if he really tried. A year and a half after graduation, Mark looked happy, fit, and truly engaged in his life. He is not only a card-carrying member of the Hooters Tour, which I understand equates to making the minor leagues in professional baseball, but has placed in his first tournament. Mark did the work it took to become a professional. Are you ready to do the same?

Play Your Own Game

The Shulas, father Don and son Dave, are an example of a father and son in the same business with a son who has truly written his own script. Don Shula, retired coach of the Miami Dolphins, is one of the most successful coaches in the history of professional football and has been inducted into the Pro Football Hall of Fame. His son Dave started out at the bottom in football and earned his credibility.

By the time Dave was 11, Coach Don Shula had his son painting blocking sleds and practice field goalposts, doing the team's laundry, and carrying out ball boy duties. By the time Dave was 16, he had graduated to charting plays and keeping statistics. Dave went from being a professional football player to being a receivers coach with the Dolphins, working alongside his dad when the team played in the Super Bowl against the Washington Redskins. He became head coach with the Cincinnati Bengals, becoming the youngest head coach of a professional football team in the modern era.

Dave Shula seems like a member of the next generation who has the talent, passion, and credibility to succeed. He currently serves as the President of Shula's Steak Houses, a successful chain of restaurants that his father founded. During his time there, he has helped the company expand to reach an international market.

The Two-Prong Approach to Career Planning

In my class, when I ask students what success means for them, they often say, "I just want to be happy." "That's good," I say, "But what does happy mean?" They'll pause, ponder, and finally say, "Happiness means being successful." Let me offer a more concrete definition of success. Success is having a career that aligns who you are and what you value with the best benefits the market has to offer.

The best way to find this career is to take a two-pronged approach. First, make an internal assessment of your personality and values. Next, couple that internal assessment with an external assessment of whether you are qualified for the careers that the marketplace is offering.

The interesting part of this process is the self-assessment part. Few college students address the task of reflecting on who they are and what they really want, and very few adults ever get to it. As you look at your personality and values over time, they do not change very much. Learning about those internal factors tends to be grounding. As you encounter and assess a new career option, you can do that assessment in the context of your fairly steady personality and values.

For example, one of the first students to graduate from my university with a minor in family business has switched her career a few times. However, those changes were grounded in her core value, which is to help people while working in a collegial atmosphere. If, down the road, someone wants her to become a tax advisor or computer programmer, she knows that is not her path to success. Note that it's okay to change your mind. However, it's important to be sufficiently grounded in your identity so that you don't shift your focus every time an exciting person, salary, or opportunity comes along.

Once you know what your values are, you can determine which careers fit those values. As early in college as possible, determine what skills, credentials, and experiences you will need at graduation to qualify for the career you choose. Career Services or your local library are good resources for this kind of information. A good idea is to shadow someone or do an internship in the career you're considering before you commit to it. Make sure you consider what benchmarks (see Chapter 4) will confirm whether you are meeting your criteria for success.

Chapter 13 deals with the internal aspects of finding a career path by explaining how to complete the McCann Action Plan for Life. You will look at your values, both in terms of how you do things and the outcomes you want in your life. From that you will be able to craft a personal definition of success. You can then use this definition as a test to assess any decision in your life, especially career choices. It becomes the rudder to help you decide what direction you want to head. Even if the winds of change, opportunity, and luck still exert a big influence, you are still guiding the ship.

Chapter 14 deals with the external aspects of finding your ideal career. This chapter explains how to build on the work in your life plan and be able to think through and effectively present the skills, credentials, and experiences you will need to be qualified to get your ideal job.

The starting point for all of this work is your attitude. Realize that no one else cares about your career as much as you need to, nor should they. Ownership means that the primary responsibility lies with you.

Find an Advisor

You have to do the hard work of choosing a career yourself, but it makes sense to seek help. I recommend finding a mentor outside of your immediate circle of family and friends who can provide support, feedback, and even advice when you need it. I also am a big believer in hiring professionals who have helped others deal with the issues and transitions that you are currently dealing with. Why not benefit from the help of someone who has helped dozens of others through the same stuff?

Many students can get most of the help they need from the Career Services department at college or maybe by just reading or researching issues online. However, just as you might get a coach to help you learn how to play a better game of golf, you may want to talk with a counselor regarding your self-assessment issues, a career counselor regarding which careers best fit you, or a life coach regarding any or all of these issues. During my life, I have used all of these professionals.

Continued

Continued

When seeking help from an advisor, follow these tips:

• Remember that the attitude of ownership is vital-you still have to do the heavy lifting.
• Talk to people who have worked with the person you are considering and trust your intuition. These types of relationships require trust and compatibility to work.
• Set some clear expectations about why you are engaging this person, your role in the process, and benchmarks to help you both see whether things are working.

The Three Players Plan for a Career

Now that you realize that neither your parents nor anyone else are responsible for your future, you have to step up and take ownership of it. Once you do, you will probably agree with one of my students who said, "I feel a lot less pressure because I have done the work to get a sense of direction. But I also feel a lot more pressure, because now I have to act on it." Once you come to this realization, the big task is to learn to write your own script and make a plan for your life and career. The following sections describe how Tony, Selina, and Pat are doing in college with that challenge.

The Amateur

Tony has no clear direction for a career or his life for that matter. If his parents want him to be a lawyer in the family business, his aunt thinks information technology is a great field, or if he really likes his poetry professor, these influences become the primary basis for picking or switching careers. This constant change creates a lot of stress. Also, his constantly changing mind has created frustration and expense (in terms of energy, money, and time) and makes people doubt his credibility.

Tony says he is going to law school, but with his C average, that seems unlikely. He hasn't yet looked at himself and his situation honestly enough to admit that he isn't going to commit to the hard work it takes to become a lawyer. By avoiding taking ownership for his life and not getting to work, Tony is setting himself up to fail. He is also establishing a reputation of being someone who lacks credibility, which means people are far less likely to want to invest any time to help him.

How does he do on the three-point analysis? He has not faced his emotional resistance because he has not even begun to look at himself. He has neither an understanding of his own personality nor a clue as to his own values, so how can he hope to match his personality and values up with a career? Can you see why he is at risk for being swayed into any career that sounds interesting?

He has not really talked with his family about what they expect, either. He doesn't know whether they want him to have the same grades, type of law school, and outside experience that the other lawyers in his parents' firm bring to the table. On the Applied Intelligence side, Tony risks being perceived as ungrounded and immature. People know his plan for a career is as likely to change as the weather. Consequently, people find it hard to take him seriously. Like a ship without a rudder, he is apt to go whichever way the wind blows.

 ## The Semipro

Selina realizes that it's important to figure out what to do for a career by including her core values and the elements that define success for her, yet she can't quite figure out how to do that. She is pretty sure that she does not want to start out right out of college in her family's business as a restaurant manager. Her older sister did that, and she doesn't seem happy. Still, she is not sure she likes her major field, which is accounting.

Some days, it seems accounting would be the best route to escape from her dad's control. However, she's having trouble committing to it, whether from lack of knowledge, failing to fully develop certain skills, or just finding it hard to get motivated for anything that seems so far off.

On the three-point analysis, Selina gets credit for starting to look at her values and her definition of success. She wants to figure out who she is and what she wants, but she's not quite there yet. She may be encountering emotional resistance and having difficulty finding resources. With her family, she still struggles with acting as a fully independent adult. As far as her Applied Intelligence goes, Selina is perceived as trying to choose a satisfying career, but not yet succeeding. Selina is running away from something she knows she does not want. Her struggle is to figure out what it is she wants and to run toward it.

The Professional

Pat is part of that elite 3 percent of adults who have assessed themselves, their family, and their family business and have defined what success is for them. She knows how to analyze a career and knows the secret to success is to match what the market (including her family's business) values with what she values. She realizes that she is not meant to start out in her family's business. She did an internship in a firm that works managing the assets of wealthy families, mostly family businesses. That experience helped her see how her personality and values aligned with a career. This view does not mean that everything will work out perfectly, nor does it mean that Pat can't change her mind. It does mean that her choices are grounded in two fundamental things that change little over a person's lifetime: values and personality.

The payoff of all of Pat's hard work shows in the three-point analysis. She gets very high marks for completing her own life plan, which included a section on self-assessment, a values-based definition of success, and a two-part analysis of her chosen career. The analysis includes linking her personality and values with her career, as well as looking at what skills, credentials, and experiences she will need at graduation. Her Applied Intelligence is high; she is perceived by others as a mature young woman who knows what she wants and can clearly articulate why she wants it and what steps she is taking to get it.

Conclusion

If you have been applying what you've read, you have done a great deal of work in this chapter. You have made a major shift from just thinking about your career to beginning what maybe 3 percent of the adults in this country ever do: creating a written life plan for yourself. You have a better understanding of who you are, what you value, and what success means to you. Chapters 13 and 14 explain this planning and assessment process in more detail, but first there are three more risks to tend to.

Keep these ideas in mind as you begin to take ownership of choosing a satisfying career:

- No one else can nor should care as much about your career as you do.
- The process of choosing a career starts with looking at yourself before you look at careers.
- Given how often everyone switches careers today, knowing how to select a career that you enjoy is an important lifelong skill.
- The career selection process has two parts: self-assessment and research into the requirements of available careers.

CHAPTER 10

Challenge 6: Including the Family Business in Your Education

Preparing for a career requires a big investment of time, money, and effort. According to the College Board, a four-year private education can easily cost between $100,000 and $150,000. Add to that investment the hundreds, if not thousands, of hours invested in course work, homework, internships, and other resume-building tasks. Yet no matter how extensive your training is, your education is incomplete if it does not address your family business values.

To help you overcome this challenge, this chapter will help you

- Gain an understanding of what role college can play in managing the opportunity your family business represents.
- Learn how college can undermine or support your efforts to earn credibility and gain marketability.
- Provide your parents with a more informed perspective on college relative to your education and the family business.

If you have already finished college, you will need to do the work of educating yourself about family business issues because they will affect your decisions about your career and your life. Reading this book and doing the work it suggests is a good start, but you should also explore other family business resources (see list in Appendix A), enlist the support of family members and mentors, and ask advice from family business professionals.

Why Your Education Should Include Your Family Business

You and your family will invest a ton of time, money, and effort into a college education. You should make sure it helps you address your biggest career issue, which is whether or not you should be involved with the family business. If you do decide to be involved with the family business, your college education should help you determine when, how, and why you should be involved. To help you understand this topic, I am going to tell you a little bit about my time in college and about the development of the Stetson University Family Business Center, which began in 1998.

My College Years

Growing up in a family that owned and operated businesses was a core part of my youth. I spent every summer from the time I was 11 until I was 20 working in one of my family's businesses. I developed a strong work ethic, a sense of independence, and a lot of credibility not only with others, but also with myself.

In the fall of 1978, I went away to a small university in Ohio. I wanted to major in accounting, and I wanted to go from there to law school. During my freshman year, changes in my family's business caused my family to relocate from Pittsburgh, Pennsylvania to West Palm Beach, Florida. The first year at the college in Ohio made me realize that not only was getting out of the cold, midwestern winters appealing, but staying connected to the family and the business had some draw for me as well. During Christmas break that year I looked at private universities in Florida that had strong accounting programs and law schools. Stetson University was the one that fit the bill, so I transferred to Stetson.

Although my family owned a business, during my four years in college the family business topic never came up. I believe there was not a college in the nation back in the late 1970s that was helping undergraduates address family business issues. If there were, it might have helped me with situations I encountered. For example, when I was a college senior, one job interviewer, an aggressive and arrogant man, asked me if I could get a job outside of my family's business. He asked it in a less-than-diplomatic manner, but he brought up an important issue, marketability, that everyone in a family who owns a business must address.

I graduated with a degree in accounting. At the time, every graduate in Stetson's accounting program had at least one job offer, and I was lucky enough to have several from the large accounting firms. At the time, I decided I didn't want to continue on to law school right away (although I went to law school later). I interviewed for and got the job I thought I wanted. However, after less than two years with a top accounting firm, I came to see that accounting was totally wrong for me given my personality and values. I could no more achieve what I would come to define as success through an accounting career than I could bake a pie out of rocks. I would be using the wrong ingredients. I hadn't done the work to make myself marketable in a career that I wanted.

My Time in the Family Businesses

At 23, I was very unhappy in my career in public accounting and ready to leave. The controller at my father's company home office (this was a firm of about 700 people with offices in several states and overseas) said the company needed an accountant. I interviewed with about half a dozen firms and my family's business seemed like the best place to work. Through luck, circumstances, and the foresight of my father, I was quickly shifted out of accounting into a new area.

I was a little like Selina in the last chapter. I was running from something, but not yet clear on what to run toward. My next step was to join my family's fairly large health care company. I had come in with a fair amount of credibility from working for years as a youth in the business. Also my degree, CPA license, and experience working for Price Waterhouse all helped show I was qualified and willing to work hard. In my new position, I worked to help get licenses for new hospitals for the company. That involved some technical research, some writing, some coordination of efforts with outside law firms, and even some public speaking and networking. I went from just being happy not to be in the impersonal, technical world of public accounting to really starting to thrive in parts of my career. Two years later, at age 25, I had the opportunity to go to law school, and this time I jumped at it. I talked with my family, and we decided that it was a good point for me to leave the family business.

When I graduated from law school, I had a great chance to become what I thought I truly wanted to be: an entrepreneur. My father, a brother, and I went into business together, which lasted for about two years. It was a great venture, but it just wasn't for me. I didn't have enough passion for it. Also, with only three of us in this small business and all of us being family, managing the family involvement was much more difficult. My younger brother and I got along great as brothers before and after this period, but we had work styles that clashed. I was almost 30 years old by then and started looking at ways to move on. After some soul searching, careful planning, and completing my version of a life plan, I finally found a career I loved: college professor. I became a college professor at Stetson University in 1990 at the age of 30 and have loved teaching ever since.

From the time I graduated college in 1981 until 1998 when I became director of the Stetson University Family Business Center, I am not sure how much I thought about the fact that my family owned businesses. I had no sense of what my family's involvement in a business meant for me and my career. Most people, even those who run family businesses or advise them, may have a lot of experience with family businesses, but they still do not have the informed perspective you now possess.

The Stetson University Family Business Center

In the summer of 1998, the dean of the business school approached me. I had been on the faculty for eight years by then, and the college had brought in a family business consultant to start a program. He had been there a year, and it had not worked out. The dean wanted me to take on the task. I'm a big believer in both learning from others and in planning, so I did three things in the center's first few years that made a big difference. First, I set up a survey of the students on campus. Would you believe that about 33 percent of the nonbusiness majors and more than 40 percent of the business majors came from families that owned businesses? What a revelation!

Second, I had a three-year strategic plan written up for the Family Business Center. (You can see I practice what I preach.) In the interest of *transparency*, the plan was available for anyone on campus to see. Transparency means allowing people to see and understand an organization's decision-making and planning processes. Both the planning and the transparency gave the Family Business Center significant credibility.

> **KEYWORD:** Transparency is when something is done in a manner that enables people to know how it is done. For example, when a family member is hired, all the other employees might be informed that she was interviewed by two nonfamily employees and held to the same standards as all the other candidates.

Third, beginning less than a year after I became director, I invited some of the top family business leaders, professors, and consultants in the nation to critique the Family Business Center's approach to helping students from families that owned businesses. From that feedback, the Family Business Center staff created a book, which included a chapter on what students like you, their parents, and other key stakeholders felt about what the center was doing. The Family Business Center sent that book to the dean of every accredited business school in the United States. So far, it has distributed over 2,000 of them to other interested people, particularly those at universities.

Doing that research, I learned that for students whose parents own a business, especially if their parents founded it, their biggest career decision involved managing the opportunities offered by having a family business available to them. I learned that a family business doesn't just force the decision about whether to move into the business at graduation, but that it also required managing the three lifelong relationships of family member, potential employee, and potential heir or owner.

If the college you attend does not help you address these issues, then you and your family are not getting your money's worth. Not only that, your education may encourage you to fall prey to the unique risks that you, as a member of a business-owning family, will face as you manage your career decisions.

A Family Business Education Policy

In a *Family Business Magazine* online newsletter (May 15, 2006), one of the most well-known consultants in the family business field, David Bork, said a family business ought to have an education policy, one that distinguished the educational requirements needed to become an owner from those needed to become an employee. So here is one of the nation's top advisors telling families who own businesses that they should inform the next generation that education is important for entry into the business.

The world's largest tree-trimming company already has just such an education policy in place. Founded in 1928, the Asplundh Tree Expert Company is family owned and operated and is moving toward its fourth generation of family leadership. Members of the fourth generation will be required to have outside work experience before entering the family business. Even members of the third generation who want to work in top management have to complete an eight-year development program. The management of this company realizes that you need to think of your education and development in terms of your family business.

Why Your Credibility Is at Risk

Other students, those who are not from family businesses, face positive pressure to get good grades; to build up their resume with clubs, internships, and awards;

and to prepare to be marketable. To do this, they usually know that they have to become more credible along the way.

For you, however, the biggest challenge may be to make college a part of helping you have a better future. Instead, you go to college assuming, and perhaps even being told by your family, that how you do in college doesn't really matter. Because you have a guaranteed job waiting for you, you don't have to worry about those things that so preoccupy the other students.

Does the term *entitlement* leap to mind here? With that attitude, you actually lower your self-esteem or at least your credibility. Because you think you are entitled to a job in the family business without earning it, you may not work toward the grades, the experiences, the skills, or the credentials to be marketable. What a waste of time college is, in that case! Please don't waste your time or your or your parents' money by being corrupted by the opportunity that your family's business represents.

Prepare and Plan for your Career

I think the 1995 movie **Tommy Boy**, starring David Spade and the late Chris Farley, does a great job of showing how not to end up after college graduation. Tommy is the son of an auto parts company owner. His dad, Big Tommy, hires his incompetent son. Tommy is likeable, but he took seven years to get through school and managed to graduate with no skills, no talent, no credibility, and no marketability.

Big Tommy dies suddenly, leaving the family firm in danger of collapse. It is up to Tommy to keep the company going and save the jobs of the townspeople who work there. Up to this point, the story line is pretty realistic. Our amateur player, Tony, could well find himself in this type of situation.

However, this is a comedy, and it has to have a happy ending. Tommy's quirky, somewhat obnoxious behavior somehow helps him to become a brilliant

Continued

Continued

salesperson and save the day. Unfortunately, real life is seldom so wonderful. Don't waste your time, your parents' money, and your credibility and marketability. Commit to something while you are in college. If your college years are behind you, make a plan to increase your credibility and marketability in a career that matches your values.

How Family Business Fits into Education

According to the Family Firm Institute, only about 100 of the thousands of universities in the United States have any type of *family business program*. Of those colleges, two dozen or so have family business courses, about three have minors, and only two allow students to major solely in family business. One of the family business major programs is at Stetson University, where I teach. The second one, which started in the fall of 2006, is at Carson-Newman College in Jefferson City, Tennessee, a college that I was fortunate enough to work with.

KEYWORD: A **family business program** is a university-based program that uses a combination of teaching, research, and the university's community outreach efforts to help families in business.

Family business programs and centers started at a few colleges in the mid-1980s. They tended to start out by putting on seminars for family businesses in the community. Few programs did much actual teaching or research on the topic, and few university-based programs addressed anyone in the next generation other than the middle-aged successor.

At the same time, many of the professionals who helped or advised family businesses, such as lawyers, accountants, and insurance people, mainly worked with the older generation on straightforward business issues and succession planning. Not many did much to address the family business holistically, and even fewer gave much guidance to the next generation.

However, as reported by Michelle DeMoss in the article "Developing Consumer-Driven Services in University-Based Family Business Programs" in the academic journal *Family Business Review* (June 2002, Volume 15, Number 2), a survey at Stetson that revealed a high percentage of students came from family businesses has been repeated by at least one other private college and one private high school. They found similar percentages.

The Family Firm Institute also cites these statistics:

- More than 80 percent of all businesses in North America are family businesses.
- One out of every 10 households owns a business.
- Family businesses account for half the number of jobs in the United States.
- Over the next 20 years, almost all family-owned businesses will lose their primary owner to death or retirement. These losses will lead to the largest intergenerational transfer of wealth in U.S. history.

With these sorts of numbers, you have to wonder why there isn't more being done at colleges for the next generation in family businesses.

Academia tends to be slow to adopt change. I think in a decade or two most colleges will have programs in family business or will at least address those issues somewhere in their curriculum. I also bet that Career Services offices will develop special programs for family business students. Once colleges appreciate the importance of this issue, they will rethink everything from textbooks to internships and recruiting fairs.

In the meantime, however, what does the current landscape of family business programs mean to you and your family? I will go out on a limb here and assume you don't want to hold off on college for 10 or 20 years. So what can you do today? I would suggest you consider two options. You can try to handle your family business issues alone and attend a college that does nothing with family business, or you can find one that helps you manage the opportunities and risks you are facing.

Because some of you will consider the first path, I will comment on it. One night I was at a cocktail party with some family business folks, and one started telling another about a program for the next generation that was a day long and cost about $400. It may have been great. But if it was only eight hours long, how could it compare to the potential benefits of a four-year program in college? I just remember asking some of the folks at this cocktail party, "Wouldn't it make a heck of a lot more sense to have all of this family business stuff be part of college?" I encourage you to seek out resources from books like this one, from consultants, and even from support networks (see the list of additional resources in Appendix A). But realize that you won't get as much out of them as you would a full four-year college family business program.

What should college do to help you? You and your family should assess which college best suits your needs, and the topic of family business should be part of that equation. Look at the Web site www.ffi.org for the Family Firm Institute's list of university-based family business programs. See which ones have courses, a minor, or a major in family business or family enterprise. See how well the program aligns with what you want, how much it will enhance your credibility, and how it fits the other criteria outlined in the following section.

What to Look for in a Family Business Program

As the director of Stetson University's Family Business Center from 1998 until 2006 and 2010 to present, I have seen first-hand the big benefits of a family business program. The students in the program gain credibility and marketability and have a four-year discussion with both their peers and their family. The following are some key features of the Stetson University family business program:

- **The McCann Action Plan for Life.** To help develop credibility, students create a 30- to 50-page life or development plan in the first family business course they take as a freshman or sophomore. Going through that process builds a sense of self-confidence. (Chapter 13 discusses this process in detail.)
- **An internship in a different family business**. Students get feedback and should aspire to get a job offer by working outside their family's business.

- **A portfolio.** In the last family business course, students develop, an extensive portfolio to demonstrate that they have the skills, credentials, and experiences they need to get the jobs they want. (Chapter 14 explains how to develop a portfolio.)
- **Family involvement**. Over the course of the four-year program, students talk to their families about family business issues. They interview family members, create genograms (family trees), and involve the family in many assignments. Families can even attend retreats to catch up on the material that their sons and daughters have been learning.

Not every college does it the same way, and not every student needs the same things, but this list gives you an overview of the kinds of things you should look for in a family business program.

How to Help Your Parents Help You

As you look at colleges, involve your parents in your process. Show them this chapter and show them the following questions to provide them with an informed perspective on how college relates to your relationship with the family business. Make it clear that you want to attend a college that will help you make the most of the next four years, help you manage this tremendous opportunity they are presenting to you, and help you become credible and marketable.

Use your college search as a starting point for your own long-term discussion with your parents about what you and they hope the next four years and beyond hold for you. Ask them what would help you enhance your credibility and marketability between now and graduation. See how they feel about you doing an internship outside the family business, or even how they feel about you starting your career outside the family business. It may be a little awkward to talk about these issues now, but it is far easier than waiting until it's time for you to make a decision about your career.

Ask These Questions Before Enrolling

You and your parents should ask the colleges you are considering the following questions:

- What percentage of your business majors come from families that own businesses?
- What percentage of your trustees are from family businesses?
- How many courses do you have in family business?
- What percentages of your business faculty have done research in family business?
- What seminars, workshops, programs, or speaker series do you offer?
- How can the rest of the family get involved with your family business program?
- What benefits can I expect from your family business program?

The Three Players Face College

Let's go back in time for this challenge to the beginning of the players' senior year in high school. Like many students across the nation, the three players have begun their search for a college.

The Amateur

Tony never really understands that a college education links to a career with or beyond his family business, so he thinks his courses and grades don't matter. Like many amateurs, Tony thinks he already knows everything that he needs to know and that college is a waste of time. Tony doesn't do a preparation course or anything else to help his SAT score, so he doesn't do well on his tests. He only considers two colleges, and those are ones his buddies are attending. He doesn't know what else to look for in assessing a college. He has done very little to make the next four years of his life worth the time, effort, and money.

Even as a high school senior, Tony has begun to be perceived as someone who talks a great game but doesn't have much substance. He has not even begun to think of his life as his responsibility. He has had no direct, honest conversations with his folks about what it would take to *earn* a position at the family law firm. He hasn't received much feedback from anyone outside the family either.

On the three-point analysis, Tony comes up short. He has not dealt with his emotional resistance of realizing that at 18 there may be a great deal he has yet to learn and that he needs to take responsibility for his future. As you have seen in other chapters, Tony and his folks think he is entitled to a job regardless of his grades or experience. With that attitude, college ultimately becomes a waste of time. He also falls pretty short on the Applied Intelligence test. People view him as being able to talk the talk, but not walk the walk. Years from now, Tony is likely to be unhappy in his career and to regret this approach to college.

The Semipro

Selina wants to link the educational process with the option of going into the family business, even to the point of considering whether to start in her parents' business or an outside firm. However, no one on the campuses she visits seems ready, willing, or able to help. She struggles to find a college, but she hears from the teachers, career services people, and even the textbooks that everyone is destined for a career in a large publicly traded company like IBM, Proctor & Gamble, or Intel. As a semipro, she often feels like she is dealing with this issue all alone or at least separately from the rest of her college career.

Selina's feelings are understandable. Few colleges have done much to help students like her who come from family business backgrounds. Fortunately, that is changing, and there are programs to consider and good questions to ask.

On the three-point analysis, Selina gets good marks for addressing her emotional resistance and trying to find help with managing the opportunity of her family business. In terms of talking with her family, she doesn't even realize yet that her journey will include not only talking with her folks, but also starting to make her own decisions. In terms of Applied Intelligence, Selina is perceived as a somewhat typical confused young student who is trying to figure out things.

The Professional

Pat realizes that making the choice whether or not to enter the family business is her biggest college and career decision. She decided it was important when selecting a university to determine whether it offered courses in family business to help inform that decision. She figures that if she and her family are going to invest over $100,000 and four years in a college education, that education should help her address these family business issues.

Pat chooses to go to a college that offers a major in family business. It is a small private college, which her parents like. It has other strong business majors, too, so students can major in one field of business while getting either a minor or a second major in family business. These offerings appeal to Pat. The programs include the family both in the course work and with retreats and seminars. As a result of attending an open house event on campus, Pat and her parents talked about some important family issues.

Pat is starting off on the right foot, and the three-point analysis shows that. She has taken ownership in selecting a college and found one that addressed her needs. She has involved her parents in the selection process, and they have already begun to see that Pat wants to take a leadership role in determining her own future. Pat will discuss important issues with them, and she wants their support, but she also wants to become her own person. In terms of her Applied Intelligence, Pat is off to a strong start.

Conclusion

The challenge presented in this chapter is to make college part of successfully managing the opportunity your family business represents. As part of college, you should start to address your biggest career decision: if, when, how, and why should I become involved with my family's business? (Of these questions, the why is the most important.) Also, keep in mind the three lifelong relationships you will have to manage: family member, potential employee/leader, and potential owner/heir. In addition, you should consider whether the college you attend will undermine or support your efforts to earn credibility and gain marketability.

Finally, be aware that family business needs to be part of your vision for long-term professional development. From getting your MBA to continuing education and in-house training and throughout your professional development, you will need to take into consideration the fact that you are a part of a family that owns a business.

Remember these key points from the chapter:

- Make sure that the university you attend has a program to help you deal with your family business issues. Most importantly, the college you attend should help you to become credible and marketable.
- Because everything affects everything else in a family business, the work you do in college needs to involve your family.
- Bear in mind you will need to consider the family business in all of your education, training, and professional development in the future.

PART IV

Confronting the Ongoing Challenges in Your Career

This part looks at the challenges that you will face after college. In Chapter 11, you learn about the seventh challenge: getting trapped in your family business. Suppose you were hired by your family business in an act of charity instead of as a result of having impressive set of skills. You are probably overpaid and have a lifestyle that demands your current inflated salary. You are afraid to leave because you think you aren't good enough to get hired by another company at the position you have and the salary you make in the family business. Here's the scary part: You are probably right.

Chapter 12 deals with the eighth and final challenge: how to get reliable feedback. Though this issue will be with you throughout your life, I put it last because it is even more important after college. Also, I want you to think specifically about feedback after you have read most of this book. By the time you get to Chapter 12, you will be much more informed, motivated, and aware of why and in which areas you most need to seek feedback.

CHAPTER 11

Challenge 7: Avoiding the Golden Handcuffs

T he parents of a student I knew were willing to pay him about $80,000 to come home right out of college and manage the family restaurant. His resume didn't justify that salary. He was probably worth about half that in the marketplace. Yet he found it too hard to resist and joined the family business.

If you had such an offer would you take it? One of the skills I want to help you develop in this chapter is the ability to look down the road at the consequences of your choices, especially the offer from your family's business. I want you to avoid ending up feeling trapped.

By the end of this chapter, you will be able to

- Understand and appreciate the risk of being caught in golden handcuffs.
- Realize why the work that you are doing now can address this future challenge.
- Start to take the steps to avoid getting caught in the golden handcuffs.

Joining Your Family Business for the Right Reasons

All members of the next generation face the challenge of making sure they work for the family business only for legitimate reasons. If you join your family's business for less than legitimate reasons, you risk getting trapped by the benefits of your job, caught in a pair of *golden handcuffs*.

KEYWORD: Golden handcuffs describes being trapped in a position in your family business by the undeserved benefits the job gives you. Because you haven't earned them, other companies in the marketplace won't match them. Thus you feel stuck, because if you leave you will probably have to take a cut in pay and status and have to increase your accountability.

The gold, in this case, is the excessive compensation you receive relative to your qualifications and your output. The handcuffs represent how trapped you will feel in this situation. Because you are overpaid, probably underqualified, and not even held fully accountable, you couldn't find another job that would match what your family has given you. If you leave, you would almost certainly make less money, have less power, and be more accountable for your performance. Would you want to be 30, married with children, and facing this challenge for the first time? Or would you rather address it now?

If you work for your family's business when you aren't qualified to do so, you will lack credibility. And if you don't have to meet the same performance goals as other employees and if you are overpaid for what you do, you will not earn credibility. As a consultant, I've seen that although many people envy a person in this position, that person is often the least happy person in the family and in the business. Why? Such people make a lot of money and do nothing—must be nice, right? But most employees can spot these amateurs a mile away and will avoid going to them with decisions, ideas, or for advice. They themselves feel like frauds, because they typically know they aren't getting these benefits because they deserve them, but because the family is giving them a gift they did not earn.

The prices for such "gifts" include lowered self-esteem and a feeling of hopeless entrapment, which accompany lowered credibility and lowered marketability. The marketplace will not offer them a job equivalent to the one they have, so they are constantly afraid of being let go and having to take a more demanding job and live on a smaller salary. This situation can be even more stressful for those living beyond their means. If you already spend more than you make (and thus have probably run up some debt), the idea of lowering your standard of living is even more threatening.

Such a deal might look good at first, but selling your credibility is a tough way to get a job. Do you think people in that position thought about the future consequences? Do you think you should?

An Offer He Should Have Refused

Some family businesses can feel more like a trap than others. In *The Godfather: Part II*, the 1974 sequel to 1972's *The Godfather*, Michael Corleone (played by Al Pacino) is now running the family business, which just happens to be organized crime. In the first film, he was seen as the son least likely to succeed his father. When his father dies with no succession plan nor heir apparent, however, Michael apparently rises to the occasion. In this second film, Michael feels more and more trapped by his position. In his case it may not be the money keeping him in place—I am sure anyone running a criminal organization must feel like it is awfully difficult to get out. At one point his wife says, "You once told me in five years the Corleone family will be completely legitimate. That was seven years ago." Michael responds, "I know. I'm trying, darling." Sounds pretty trapped to me.

Deciding Whether to Work Somewhere Else First

One of my brothers started working in our family business directly out of college. It was a small startup company, which I imagine made it even more difficult. His only supervisor was a family member, our father. At the time, Dad also was running a large health care company, so he had only limited time to provide structure, guidance, and feedback to my brother. In addition, my brother started out working out of a home office, which adds a layer of difficulty for anyone but especially someone in his first job. Starting in this situation right out of college, I think that he always had a tougher time feeling credible inside the company and being clear on what he might do if he ever wanted to leave.

I started outside my family's business in the public accounting firm of Price Waterhouse. Even though I had chosen a career that didn't really work out for me, having outside experience helped my credibility in the family business, as did having a nonfamily employee in my father's healthcare business recruit me to join the family business.

Most experts in the field of family business will tell you that it is far easier, and usually better, to start your career outside your own family business. Both Stetson University's family business major and minor actually require an internship in a family business besides the student's own or with a firm that advises family businesses.

If you go directly from college into your family business, the hard part of the golden handcuffs challenge isn't over. You still have to earn and protect your credibility and your marketability. That is what people who end up feeling trapped don't realize. They imagine they're being offered a better position with higher compensation than they could get anywhere else. That offer sounds great, but there's a serious downside.

I once met with a lawyer who had hired his two sons directly out of law school. He talked with me for a few hours. He felt frustrated because, as he put it, his sons didn't know how good they had it. He said they were paid more than the market value for their services, probably worked fewer hours, and were under less pressure than they would be in most law firms. Because they had never worked anywhere else, I asked him, "How *could* they know how good they had it?" He realized they had no context for that understanding, and if he tried to tell them, he would just sound like a father and not like a boss.

Working outside the family business first gives you greater self-confidence because you have a context for how other firms function. My first week at my family's small business, my brother and I put in a 40- to 45-hour week. My brother felt that was a long week, a lot of hours. But after working for the large accounting firm and my family's larger business and going through final exams in law school and busy seasons in an accounting firm, it didn't seem that tough to me. I had a broader context gained from more outside experience.

Going into your family business, especially right out of college, should be the tougher choice, not the easier one. Outside experience gives you that broader context and insight into how other firms operate. You might grow to appreciate how generously or even how unfairly your parents treat you. You might see how much technology, outside consultants, or other new ideas could add to your family business. All this knowledge improves not only your self-confidence, but also others' perceptions of you, which is the external aspect of credibility.

Before you commit to joining the family business, follow these suggestions to protect your credibility:

- Get two outside job offers from other firms.
- Don't accept a salary or position for more than the highest of your two offers.
- Don't accept a salary or position higher than your resume would justify.
- If possible, have a nonfamily supervisor.
- Make sure you have written performance reviews at least every six months.
- Develop an exit strategy that allows either the family or you to end the employment relationship while protecting the family relationship.

Involving Your Family in the Decision

I've said that in a family business everything affects everything. Often parents conspire in creating a golden handcuffs situation. I have had parents tell me they will gladly pay their children far more than any salary they are offered just to make sure they join the family business.

Members of the next generation who get caught in the golden handcuffs and end up leaving the family business, whether voluntarily or involuntarily, often do so in a way that hurts their relationship with the family.

Now is the time to start having discussions with your family about these issues. Begin by talking about your family's expectations for your entering the family business and asking these questions:

- What are the skills, credentials, and experiences you would need to get the job if you were not a family member?
- How will your performance be evaluated and by whom? Can you have a nonfamily supervisor and written reviews?

Many of my students ask their families for a written job offer. If your folks don't provide one, draft one and show it to the family.

Finally, take some time and talk about how either the family or you could end the employment relationship. What kind of exit strategy would enable you to leave or your family to let you go but still preserve the family relationship? It may be difficult to talk about these issues now, but an ounce of prevention really is worth a pound of cure.

Blue Eyes and Business Sense

Everyone knows that Paul Newman is a great actor, but did you also know that he is a family business owner? The Newman's Own brand includes such products as popcorn and salad dressing. An increasingly popular brand, Newman's Own Organics, was started by his daughter Nell.

According to the Newman's Own Organics Web site, Nell Newman grew up pursuing her passion as a dedicated environmentalist, majoring in human ecology at The College of the Atlantic in Bar Harbor, Maine, a long way from Hollywood and the movie business. She worked in various careers before joining the family business, including the Environmental Defense Fund and the Ventana Wildlife Sanctuary. Then she convinced her father to start an organic foods division of the business.

Her father addressed the challenge of the golden handcuffs by agreeing to hire her, but only paying her $15,000 for her first year of work, and that was just for expenses. In a 2005 interview with Jen Abelson for the *Boston Globe*, Nell described how her family navigated this challenge, "After our first year when we made a profit, we had to pay him back for everything, including our salaries. So if we wanted a raise, he was actually very good about it, but we had to be accountable. We were profitable our first year and have been ever since."

The Three Players Face the Golden Handcuffs

It's three years after college. Where have the three players landed and how are their careers going? How might they deal with the challenge of the golden handcuffs?

The Amateur

Tony sees the family business as his way to avoid what one student of mine called the "cliff" that graduation represented for him. He sees the family business as a ticket to bypass the stress and pressure of college, of self-assessment, of exposing yourself to rejection in the marketplace, and, to put it broadly, of growing up.

Tony is now two years out of school; he took an extra year to graduate. He applied to a number of law schools but never was accepted. For the last two years, he has worked as sort of an office manager in training under his father. He does not like it and feels trapped.

His folks pay him $45,000, which is about $15,000 more than he could have earned with his C average as a general business major. Yet Tony sees the young lawyers making over $80,000 right out of law school and he feels he ought to be making that much. He even sees that his dad makes $100,000 as the office manager and would like to make that much soon. Tony talks in terms of what he wants, not in terms of what he is worth. Other people in the firm see him as a spoiled young man who is far from credible.

Tony doesn't like his job. It is full of details and routine: collecting payments from clients, nagging attorneys to turn in time sheets, and reviewing reports and plans. He also notices that he fights more and more with his parents now that he is working for them. He and his dad now butt heads all the time, and each tends to go to Tony's mom and complain about the other. She doesn't want to be in the middle of these arguments and has blown up a few times about it. The tension at work and around his parents' house is getting worse.

The three-point analysis shows that Tony is reaping what he has sown. Tony is now living with the consequences of not dealing with his emotional resistance. He still hasn't taken ownership for his life. He still has an attitude of entitlement, has earned little credibility, and is hardly marketable at all. His parents are starting to think Tony doesn't know how good he has it. In fact, they are thinking of putting him on probation.

As far as Applied Intelligence, Tony now deserves a reputation as someone who only has and keeps a job with his family's business because of an act of charity by his family. Don't end up on this road to being a "victim" like Tony. Nobody wins in this situation, especially not Tony.

 ## The Semipro

Selina starts her career outside the family business in an accounting firm. She feels good about having the guts to not get sucked into the family business. Her mom is supportive of her decision, but her father has mixed feelings. He is proud of Selina for having the courage to go out and find her own path, yet he still believes it would be best for her to work with the family.

Selina has addressed the challenge of getting caught in the golden handcuffs. She isn't trapped, but at the same time she isn't totally happy with her accounting career either. However, she knows she is legitimately marketable. She got her job on her own because of her skills, credentials, and experiences.

She *earned* it. This knowledge helps her self-esteem and causes other people to view her as legitimate. Although she knows she still has work to do and doesn't want to get stuck in an unfulfilling accounting career, she does give herself credit for not falling into the golden handcuffs from which her older sister is trying to break free.

How does Selina do on the three-point analysis? She has dealt with one key part of her own emotional resistance. She was not seduced back into the family business as a way to avoid growing up and taking responsibility for her career and her life. On another key aspect of her emotional resistance, seeking a career that aligns with her personality and values, Selina still has work to do.

In her family dealings, Selina again gets pretty high marks. She has continued discussions about what she wants and did not accept the script her father drafted for her. She learned from her older sister's experience.

With her Applied Intelligence, she again gets a mixed score. Selina deserves high marks for following her own path, but lower marks for not doing enough work to make that path an authentic success. She has avoided the golden handcuffs, but she has not yet found her own path to a successful career.

The Professional

Pat starts her career outside her family's business. She is working in the finance department of a large family business in a nearby city. She established the connection with the company while she was an intern. The business was a client of the financial advising firm where she did her internship. The family who owned the company was very intrigued by Pat's dual majors in finance and family business.

Pat is paid well, but only because the market says she is worth it. She had one offer that was a little higher on salary, but she went with a family business that aligned with her values better. She was pretty sure she would be happier and more productive as a result.

She is not trapped in the golden handcuffs. She knows her worth in the marketplace, and she plans to continue to develop her skills and keep her options open. Be it moving up with her existing employer, entertaining offers from other firms, or even considering going back to work with her family's business, Pat has a lot of options. She is going to continue to cultivate her marketability.

You can see the momentum that Pat has is the three-point analysis. She has overcome her emotional resistance to taking ownership for her life, and it has paid off. She has taken charge of her life and not let that task fall to her family. Her Applied Intelligence is very high. People see Pat as a confident young woman who knows she has a lot to learn and is willing to ask for help, but also realizes that she is responsible for her career, her life, and her happiness.

Conclusion

The golden handcuffs are a big challenge to the next generation in family businesses. At any juncture in your career, but especially as you graduate from college, deciding whether to accept a job offer to work in the family business is something you should consider only after a lot of reflection. You do not want to end up feeling trapped in your family business with no viable options. You don't want to one day realize that all these benefits that you have gotten used to—the high salary, the important title, and the lack of accountability—were gifts from your family, not something you earned. Accordingly, no other company will ever make you the same job offer.

If you are ever forced to leave or choose to leave, you will risk losing all this and will probably have a major blow dealt to your self-confidence and credibility. You also don't want to threaten your relationships with your parents and the rest of the family if they ever have to ask you to leave the family business.

Look down the road before you make a decision to enter the family business. Consider the tips and questions in this chapter. Analyze the offer with your family member hat, your employee hat, and even your owner hat if that is relevant. It should make sense from all these perspectives. If you are only being given a job or being allowed to keep your job because you in the family then don't take it. Don't get caught in the golden handcuffs.

Remember these key points from this chapter:

- Never take a job with the family business for less than legitimate reasons. Be aware how your emotional resistance factors into your decision.
- Start talking with your family now about their expectations for your entry to and exit from the family business.
- If joining the family business, especially right out of school, seems like an easier path, *look again*. It isn't.
- Ask yourself what taking the family business job offer at this salary will do to your credibility and marketability in the long term.

CHAPTER 12

Challenge 8: Getting Objective Feedback

We all have blind spots about ourselves. Honest feedback enables us to look at our entire selves from an outside perspective. In order to effectively work on yourself, to address the other seven challenges, and to continue to develop professionally, you need to make getting feedback a core part of your practice. Feedback is vital to being able to address all the other challenges to your professional growth.

By the end of this chapter you will be able to

- Understand what feedback is.
- Give and receive positive and critical feedback to others.
- Seek out feedback from someone who is neither family nor a friend.

Holding Up the Mirror

One of my colleagues uses the great phrase "holding up the mirror" to describe giving objective feedback to someone. Giving *feedback* is a process that involves three steps.

KEYWORD: Feedback is giving or getting someone else's perspective on how a specific behavior affected themselves and/or others and then figuring out the long-term effect of that behavior if it is repeated or continued.

First, you must objectively recount the facts of situation, including the behavior on which you want to give feedback. The two critical factors in this step are to be concrete and specific while being objective. For example, to tell someone, "You are always late and a total slacker," is far too general and judgmental. To say, "You were late five times last month by at least 15 minutes each time," is much better. The first statement will only make the person defensive, but the second statement gives the person specific, concrete behaviors to evaluate and adjust.

Second, you want to discuss the effect of the behavior. The effect can be on the person to whom you are giving feedback, to others, or to you (although this won't be true if you are giving objective feedback, because objectivity dictates that the behavior does not affect you). You might tell the person who is often late that you are concerned about others judging the person to be irresponsible if he is late one out of every four days. Note that the effect can be positive as well. If, for example, a nonfamily employee makes an effort to get to know you and help you learn the ropes during your first week on the job in the family business, you can give feedback by telling him how welcome his behavior makes you feel during this stressful transition.

Third, you want to talk about the longer-term effect that behavior might have if it continues. For example, a person who is habitually late will be evaluated poorly in his next six-month evaluation, will not be eligible for a promotion, or might undermine your authority as his boss. Or you can talk about the consequences to the organization. Other people might come to feel entitled to come in late or leave early, and morale and productivity could suffer. If a person is behaving in a positive way, letting her know the potential effect of her actions can boost her confidence and motivate her to achieve greater things.

Positive and Negative Feedback

Most people avoid giving feedback, because it is hard to give. Most people are comfortable with either giving praise or giving criticism. Always giving praise enables you to avoid conflict, at least in the short run, and feel like you are being a nice, supportive person. Offering criticism can help you feel more competent and potentially improve the other person's performance. However, if you always use just one approach, people will tend to avoid your input. Constant praise tends to cost you credibility, and constant criticism tends to be draining.

The Center for Creative Leadership suggests giving four pieces of positive feedback for every critical piece of feedback. That way, you have a balance. You don't want to always be seen as positive and avoiding the difficult topics, nor do you want to always be critical, which even the strongest person will find to be discouraging.

Helpful Feedback

To illustrate how to give helpful feedback, I'll give you an example. A student of mine, a senior, came into my office one afternoon. He was facing graduation, and we talked about his future. My student was torn between going to work in his family business or going to graduate school. As we talked, he decided he was stuck. He just couldn't make up his mind. He planned to do what he had done in similar situations. He would wait until circumstances decided for him or wait until the very last minute, when he would be forced to make a decision. As you might have guessed, he had a great deal of emotional resistance.

I could have given him advice about whether he should choose graduate school or the business, but I thought feedback would be more useful to him. In an objective manner, I talked to him about his pattern of staying stuck until something came along to force his hand. I was surprised when he told me that he intended to avoid making a choice. Until that moment, I had never known anyone who was conscious of both being stuck and choosing to stay that way. We then discussed the effects of his deliberate indecision. Together, we started a list of the costs and benefits of that choice to stay stuck at a fork in the road.

Next, I pointed out the long-term impact of this pattern. By continuing it, he would not develop the skills needed to proactively make decisions, he would be less likely to get what he really wanted, and he would probably erode his credibility with others if they saw this passive approach to dealing with life's transitions.

My student thought this over for a few days and came back to my office. He had decided to become unstuck. He had actually made two decisions and had made them proactively. First, he had decided on his career path. Second, he had made a decision about how he would address major life choices from that point on. We talked about it again a month later. He realized he had stepped up to the plate and had broken a pattern in his life, and he appreciated the feedback I had given him.

Receiving Objective Feedback

One of the most important lessons I ever learned is that as you move up in an organization, the biggest risk to your career is lack of honest, objective feedback. I learned this from two leadership programs I attended at the Center for Creative Leadership, and I believe the statement is even truer in a family business. Families have so much history, emotional connection, and desire to keep the harmony that they find it extremely hard to give and to hear objective feedback from one another.

Without ongoing, honest feedback, you can gradually steer farther and farther off course. It is like driving your car with all the gauges covered up; you won't have the information you need to judge if something is going wrong. Is the engine hot? How fast are you going? Do you have enough gas? Are you due for maintenance?

Think of objective, honest feedback as the gauge for your career. Without that feedback, you may not know there is a problem until something goes catastrophically wrong. Likewise, if you surround yourself with people who act like malfunctioning gauges by giving you inaccurate feedback that your behavior is acceptable, you are more likely to blame others when things do blow up. You risk another catastrophe because you refuse to see that your behavior needs to change.

Lack of Feedback Is Risky Business

The Rigas family owned Adelphia, one of the largest cable companies in the United States. However, they didn't run it professionally. The company was forced into bankruptcy in 2002 because of the fraud the family committed and its resultant impact.

Even after the company was publicly traded and subjected to greater scrutiny by the press and regulators, the Rigas family continued to violate the boundaries between family and business, charging inappropriate personal expenses to the business and defrauding other owners. At age 80, the patriarch, John Rigas, received a 15-year prison sentence. His son received 20 years. Do you think they needed stronger objective feedback from outside the family?

Seeking Objective Feedback

If you are a family member, especially one from the next generation, then it is hard to trust praise that comes from people in the family business. Are they just being nice because you're the boss's kid? It is equally hard to believe their criticism. Are they just resentful or jealous of you? What you need is objective feedback on important career issues: Are you getting things done professionally and in a timely manner? Do you have the respect of your coworkers? Where might you benefit from a little training?

Although you should be giving and receiving feedback with someone with whom you feel comfortable, keep in mind that you probably can't get objective feedback from family or friends. Family and friends have too much history and future with you to be objective. Someone farther removed from your situation is more likely to be able to give you the perspective you need.

Also, your reaction to feedback depends on who is giving it. If your boss gives you clear, well-worded, constructive criticism, you may find it tough to take but ultimately useful. If your boss is your mom, and you have always felt that nothing you do is ever good enough for her, then the exact same words coming from her could be devastating. As a teacher or consultant, I can often tell students or family members information that they might easily dismiss or resent if it were to come from someone closer to them.

I remember one family business owner who came to campus. He was a member of the next generation and had increased the revenues of his family's business by a factor of almost 30, and then sold it. He didn't want to sell, but market reasons made it the best decision by far. When he talked with my class about struggling with his decision, he shared how a professional organization with which he was involved had been a great source of help. He could be totally candid with the people in the organization, in part because they had a confidentiality agreement just like Stetson University has in its courses. They offered him a setting where he could open up and be totally honest, so he could get the objective feedback he needed. He wanted people who were both removed from the emotional context of his situation, but had experience with making such decisions.

Beware of Phony Feedback

The 1995 movie **Billy Madison** stars Adam Sandler as a 27-year-old member of the next generation in a family that runs a successful business owning and operating hotels. His father is frustrated with Billy, who is a great example of an amateur and spends his days reading girlie magazines, drinking beer, and hanging out by the pool.

His father sees that Billy is unfit to run the family business, and he even tells Billy that he really didn't earn all the grades he received in school, because Dad bought off the teachers. Billy struggles to earn credibility by returning to school (starting in the first grade). By the end of the movie, Billy finally comes to terms with who he is and who he really wants to be, although he doesn't get the family business. In a humorous way, this movie shows how devastating it can be to not get objective feedback from your parents and your school.

Understanding Systems and Feedback

As you learned in Chapter 3, you, your family, and your family's business can all be viewed as systems. Every system, from the environment to a computer network to a family business to you, receives feedback. From a systems perspective, feedback is defined as the outside reaction to the system's output. When the system in question involves people, the system's output is called *behavior*.

When systems receive feedback, they adjust their behavior accordingly. Systems that don't involve people tend to adjust automatically. For example, if your computer is not sending out comprehensible information, the network may send an error message, and the computer either corrects itself or is disconnected from the network, the larger system. In contrast, you can hear feedback from someone and choose how you want to act based on that information.

When viewed from another perspective, a system can become a *subsystem* of a larger system. And as you may remember, in a system everything affects everything. Thus if the system that is you responds to feedback, your family's business, which is a larger system that you are a part of, will also be affected. If you choose to ignore feedback and make no adjustments to your behavior, that choice is likely to affect the systems you are a part of in a negative way because your harmful behavior continues and becomes a destructive pattern.

Reacting to Feedback

If giving objective feedback is like holding up a mirror for someone, receiving feedback is like looking into a mirror in that it allows you to step back from what is going on and possibly view things from a perspective you hadn't previously considered. Insightful feedback gives you the opportunity to *choose* how you want to act, rather than to merely react.

For example, my friend and colleague Michelle and I were doing some work on personality types. We came across information that said my personality type can overwhelm people. I said to Michelle, "Yeah, that's probably true for most, but not me."

To my surprise, she nodded her head as if to say, "Yes, you!" I thought, "Well, Michelle is a deep thinker and a real scholar, so maybe she is more easily overwhelmed than I realized. It could not possibly be me." I spent the next two weeks asking friends and coworkers at school and in my consulting whether I was sometimes overwhelming. Most of them felt that I could be overwhelming at times. I was amazed that all these people could be so wrong! (I'm exaggerating a bit here, but that is close to what I originally thought.)

After some time, I had to own the fact that I am very extroverted, like to rethink things, and am enormously energized by innovating, and these qualities can overwhelm people. After the dust settled and I had time to digest all this, I took the time to reflect on some of my choices. My department chair at the time, my boss in my teaching job, was much more tradition-oriented and comfortable with slow, incremental change and consistency. I now realized my brainstorming with someone like that would very likely leave that person feeling overwhelmed, confused, frustrated, and maybe even skeptical of me. Since then, I have been careful about when and with whom I let that innovative, overwhelming side emerge.

In addition to causing you to rethink behaviors, receiving thoughtful, objective feedback also can be powerful motivation. For example, when I attended my first leadership workshop at the Center for Creative Leadership, one of the most powerful pieces of feedback I received was that I was innovative. I had never really thought of myself as innovative. That's surprisingly typical. Many people don't realize some of their strengths until someone points them out. In my case, learning that I was innovative boosted my confidence and ambitions as the director of the Family Business Center and supported all the success that has flowed from it, including creating the nation's first major in family business.

Seek Out Useful Feedback

Follow these tips to get the most out of feedback:

- Find someone you trust and respect, who is neither a family member nor close friend, to give you feedback.
- Limit feedback to a specific topic at first, such as how you dealt with a conflict with your boss last week.
- Make sure the feedback is concrete and specific.
- Work with the person to analyze how your behavior affects others and therefore your reputation. What are the costs and benefits of your decision or behavior?
- Have the person help you consider what the outcome would be if your behavior continues and becomes a pattern.
- Accept feedback in other areas where the person feels he or she could help you.

The Three Players Find Feedback

Three years out of college and into careers, the three players deal with feedback in different ways.

The Amateur

Tony has a lot of emotional resistance to feedback, so he avoids it, which leads him to develop blind spots and bad habits and to rationalize bad behavior. He starts to believe it is okay to have a few drinks at lunch and to tell off-color jokes at work. He shows up late, leaves early, and often doesn't follow through on his responsibilities. Yet he thinks he is probably doing all right, which is a clear case of denial.

Tony never gets much real feedback, so his Applied Intelligence remains low. A few of the other employees tell him he is doing great, but he suspects they are just sucking up. A few seem to give him grief when he is bending the rules, but Tony thinks they don't understand that his family owns the company.

Tony's relationship with his parents is worsening, too. His parents keep nagging him, but he figures that they won't really do anything to him. However, his parents soon set him down and give him the bad news. They are putting him on a three-month probation working under a nonfamily employee. If he doesn't cut it, Tony will be let go.

The Semipro

Selina wants to get feedback, but she isn't sure how to go about it. Her family often tells her what they think about everything in her life. Her dad always tells her how everything, from her last boyfriend to her latest proposal for upgraded software, is not good enough. Her mom is always supportive, yet Selina wonders if there aren't some problems that Mom just won't mention.

The people Selina works with seem nice, but she is never sure if they are honest and objective. That lingering doubt is tough and has made her a little paranoid. On some days she feels full of confidence. On others, she has a whole lot of self-doubt. She just isn't sure how to accurately assess her own performance. The firm does not do formal performance reviews, and Selina is unsure how to ask for one. She has never pursued getting a mentor (her dad says he can do that for her) and feels too busy to join any professional organizations.

Selina is halfway there. She is at risk of not overcoming her emotional resistance to getting feedback, which is her biggest stumbling block. She continues to waffle on the role she wants her family to play, especially her dad. When she feels secure, she wants him to treat her like an adult, but when she is insecure, she falls back into a more dependent role. These two factors combine to hurt her Applied Intelligence. She is seen as sometimes on the ball and sometimes lost and immature. Consistency is not Selina's strong suit.

The Professional

Pat knows enough not to rest on her laurels. She has structured her life so that she gets feedback. The first thing she did in college was find a mentor. She has a colleague named Cindy in the same career but a few years further along. She and Cindy have lunch about every two weeks, and she knows that Cindy will be honest about what she sees going well and what might need Pat's consideration. Inside the firm, she seeks all the feedback she can get: performance reviews every six months, lunch with her boss, and evaluations on major projects. Because she started outside the family business, she knows her evaluations are more objective than if she had started in her parents' business.

She has even joined two professional organizations, one for family business advisors and one for women in business. She attends leadership conferences whenever possible. Pat deserves all that she has earned: the sense of self-esteem from having overcome her emotional resistance, an adult relationship with her parents, and incredibly high Applied Intelligence.

Conclusion

As you move toward applying these eight challenges to your life and to developing your own practice, feedback is a crucial way to see whether you are on track. Just like the gauges on a car, the diagnostics on your computer, or your annual physical exam, feedback on your performance is imperative to ensuring a healthy career. Feedback also is a great tool to use in order to narrow the gap between your character and your reputation and thus improve your Applied Intelligence.

Remember these key points from the chapter:

- When giving feedback, start with specific behaviors, then look at the immediate consequences of that behavior, and finally project the long-term consequences of repeating such behavior.
- Getting feedback is invaluable to your ongoing development into a professional. Not getting it is the biggest career risk to you or any professional.

Continued

Continued

- Family and friends often have a hard time providing objective feedback, and you may have an even harder time hearing their comments objectively. Seek someone a little bit removed from the situation for the best feedback.

PART V

Becoming a Professional

P art V is where you see how to apply what you've learned. In Chapter 13, I talk about a tool that since 1998 has helped change many lives of people in the next generation, the McCann Action Plan for Life. This plan is a tested and proven way to take ownership for your life and earn the credibility you want and need to succeed as a professional. I define credibility as legitimate self-confidence, which is primarily an internal feeling but includes feedback and validation from other people.

Marketability is the flip side of the coin. Chapter 14 deals with this topic by explaining how to develop a portfolio that demonstrates your marketability. Marketability means you can say and demonstrate that you have the skills, credentials, and experiences you need to succeed in a career that aligns with who you really are. You demonstrate both your credibility and marketability in your career portfolio.

CHAPTER 13

Developing a Life Plan

Since 1998, the one feature of the Family Business program at Stetson University that has received the most attention is something I developed called the McCann Action Plan (MAP) for Life. Students, parents, reporters, other universities, and employers have all been impressed and intrigued by it. The students who have gone through this process say it is the most important part of the major.

The MAP for Life can help you to take ownership of your life. It incorporates all the information in this book and links the eight challenges into a practice that will get you where you want to go *and* help you enjoy the journey to get there. It also requires a commitment of time and effort from you. Are you willing to invest 20 to 40 hours in planning your career if doing so will double or even triple your chances of success? Yes? Let's see if you are ready to become a professional and do it!

By the end of this chapter, you will be able to

- Understand the benefits of planning and people's emotional resistance to it.
- Establish a solid foundation for your life plan by completing the self-assessment and values clarification parts of the MAP for Life
- Evaluate career options by matching them with your values and doing research about what the career requires
- Link the MAP for Life with credibility and marketability

The Emotional Resistance to Planning

Based on my personal experience since 1998 of asking groups of students, family businesses, consultants, and trade associations, only about 5 percent of the adults in this country have any written plan for their life. Almost no one has anything of much depth, breadth, or deep thought.

All through my career, especially relative to family business, I have often heard people talk about all the reasons not to plan. "It takes too long," they say. They say that things change too quickly or that they don't know how to plan.

I once spent four days in a retreat with seven other family business center directors, people whose job includes preaching the virtues of planning to their family business members or students. To my surprise, only one of those seven had a working plan for their center. I recently spoke at a national convention of people in a certain industry. About 60 people in the room were from family businesses, and only 1 person out of that 60 had a plan for his business.

Very few people take time to plan, and that includes even professionals and their own businesses. Yet lack of planning is one of the key reasons businesses, including family businesses, fail. This lack of planning is also why careers fail.

Planning is hard. It can be very demanding and stressful. But that struggle produces benefits. If there is no personal growth without personal struggle, then planning is one of those tasks where whatever effort you invest will pay off in personal growth and greater self-awareness.

My clients tell me that planning has helped them to think things through and clarify what they want and how they will move toward that goal. If you look at any book on careers, family business, and even self-improvement, they will all talk about the value of planning. Would you take a hike without a destination in mind, a trail map, and a compass? Would you get on a plane without a flight plan? Planning lets you envision where you want to go. What are the chances you are going to end up where you want to go if you don't have an end in mind?

I think the real reason most people don't plan comes down to emotional resistance. Sitting down, looking toward the future, making a commitment, and feeling accountable is hard. If the planning includes self-reflection and self-analysis, it's even more difficult. But all of that is exactly what professionals do and what ownership is about.

The Benefits of the MAP for Life

The students who go through the family business program at Stetson University write a 30- to 50-page life plan as part of one of the courses I teach. I give the students an outline to follow when writing their plan. (Appendix B shows this outline in its entirety.) This outline, called the MAP for Life, consists of four main parts:

I. Self-assessment
II. Values clarification and a definition of success
III. An in-depth exploration of three of the eight family business challenges
IV. An internal and external analysis of a career

Parts I and II are the foundation, the stable part of the plan that students use to measure, manage, and maximize their life and career choices. The purpose of the MAP for Life is not to pick one career path and lock them into it forever. The MAP for Life enables them to look at the personal growth issues they want to address as they relate to the eight challenges, and it helps them look at selecting or changing a career path.

This life plan is the major project for the semester. The students have several assignments throughout the semester that directly link to it. These assignments often involve the family, in a family interview, for example. The class meets one hour per week, and students can discuss applying the course to their lives. That discussion helps them with the life plan, too. The life plan must be turned in twice, once about halfway through the semester and again near the end. Between those two dates, all students must meet with me (and Peter Begalla, my coteacher, if they want him included) at least once for at least 30 minutes to get feedback, support, and advice on their plans.

Writing a life plan is a process, not an event. No student, even some very bright ones who made college careers out of doing everything at the last minute, has ever done a good job on this project by trying to complete it in one sitting. To do it well takes time for reflection and thinking things through.

Here are some things my students have said about the benefits of writing their life plans:

- "Writing things down makes it much more real to me."
- "Writing it down shows me gaps in my thinking that I hadn't seen before."
- "Writing it down allows me to show it to others and get helpful feedback."
- "Writing my life plan allows the ideas to sink into my brain, and I started to make decisions differently."
- "I realize that if things change I can just change the plan. It actually creates more flexibility."
- "I feel less stress because my decisions are grounded in who I am and what I value."

You may not have all the help and support that students in the family business program do, but you can still get tremendous benefit from doing the work. It doesn't matter how many pages you write. What matters is how deeply and honestly you approach it. You have already read almost this entire book and done a lot of thinking, so you are further along than you may realize. An honest five-page life plan will still greatly help you and put you in a very elite group of adults. Start this process and see where it takes you. Remember the MAP for Life is not just about the outcome; it's also about the journey. It is not just about the conclusion; it's about your ability to take ownership for your life.

Parts I and II of the MAP for Life

One of the great benefits of the MAP for Life is that the first two parts, the self-assessment and the values-based definition of success, don't change much. They may shift around early on while you are figuring out who you are and perhaps again if you go through major life changes such as marriage, parenthood, or a significant loss. Yet who you are and what you value tend to be stable and grounding. They provide a rudder to help you stay on course and a way to assess any life transition, including a career change.

In 2000, Jill Shipley was the first of two people to minor in Family Business at Stetson. Jill changed her life plan many times. She saw many attractive career options and wanted to explore them all. However, Parts I and II of her plan never changed. Her passion and her definition of success were centered on teaching and helping people in a healthy and cooperative organization. She worked toward that goal in her position as the first assistant director of the Family Business Center at Stetson. She is now a very successful professional in a cutting-edge private wealth management firm that helps wealthy families. She is part of the firm's innovative effort to develop educational programs for its clients. She loves her job and is thriving, and she is still teaching and helping people.

The Self-Assessment: Who Am I?

I talked about life stages in Chapter 1. At this juncture of your life, you are probably working on figuring out who you are and what you want, as well as identifying your strengths and weaknesses. The best tool I know for doing that, one that I have been using since 1990, is the Myers-Briggs Type Indicator (MBTI). This tool is very helpful when you do the work of Part I.

The MBTI helps you to look at your preferences on four scales:

- How you focus your energy (Introversion or Extraversion)
- How you learn (Sensing or Intuition)
- How you make decisions (Thinking or Feeling)
- How you organize your life (Judging or Perceiving)

Each of these scales measures peoples' preferences on a continuum. After measuring your preferences on these four simple scales, you end up with a four-letter type. For example, if you're an ESTJ, you are extraverted, sensing, thinking, and judging.

Once you have identified your four-letter type, you can tap into a very deep reservoir of information about yourself relating to time management, study skills, family, communication, leadership, career, and your method of handling stress. You also can link this self-knowledge to family business challenges, such as developing Applied Intelligence and handling wealth and power.

Try the MBTI

The MBTI has been around for over 50 years. It is the most widely used personality instrument in the world, and it helps people see normal differences in preferences. It does not diagnose problems such depression or attention deficit disorder, but it observes and analyzes the normal, healthy differences in preferences. Going too far into the personality types is beyond the scope of this book, but there are three things you should remember about personality type:

- You, not the indicator or anyone else, decides your four-letter type.
- Just as we all use both our right and left hands, we all use both ends of each preference scale. For example, everyone has at least some characteristics of both introversion and extraversion. However, just as we tend to be either right-handed or left-handed, one end tends to dominate.
- Type does not excuse behavior. You can't just rationalize with, "Oh well, it's not my fault—I'm an extrovert".
- Remember to respect differences and expect development.
- For an easy way to take the MBTI and find your type, go to my Web site at www.familybusinesshelp.com. Realize that this test is really just an indicator of your four preferences or type. Think of it as an assessment of your preferences. Do you prefer chocolate or vanilla? Even if the assessment says you like chocolate, you know which you really prefer. Determining your type is your call!

You might also consider buying one or two of the related books listed in the appendix. My recommendation is *Type Talk* by Otto Kroeger and Janet M. Thuesen. When I do workshops or have my students learn the MBTI, I often ask people to read the description of the four scales and challenge them to see which four preferences fit them best.

Once you get a sense of your four-letter type, try it on for a while. Get some feedback from friends, family, and even a teacher. Read a little more about type and see where it fits you and where it doesn't. In the years I have used the MBTI, most people get a strong sense of their type fairly quickly. Others are usually clear on two or three of the scales and need time to ponder their preference on one or maybe two of the scales. Give yourself time to reflect, to read more, and to talk with other people to get their perspective.

My students have liked working with the MBTI very much, because it allows them to more deeply process who they are. The indicator demonstrates that each of the 16 personality types has strengths and weaknesses. Many of my students, particularly the ones who choose Thinking, learn they may have more room for development than they realized. Others, especially the ones who choose Feeling, learn they may already have more strengths than they knew. These results link with the eighth challenge of getting objective feedback. Personality type descriptions are a very objective source of understanding how people with your preferences operate and their strengths and areas for development.

If you are bold enough to start writing your life plan, begin your self-assessment by answering the following questions:

1. What is the MBTI four-letter personality type that you have selected for yourself?
2. What are your three greatest strengths and three areas that most need improvement, as they relate to your personality?
3. What are three goals that you would like to achieve in the next year?

4. For each goal, what benchmarks (list at least two) will show that you are making progress toward your goal?

5. Who would be the ideal person to give you feedback, support, and advice on this part of your plan?

A Values-Based Definition of Success

Each semester, my coteacher Peter and I have a discussion with the students about what success means to them. Some semesters, we tell students to write a page on this topic. When we give that assignment, you can feel everyone in the room panic. It is only a small assignment worth about 5 percent of their grade for that semester, but they want structure, details, and everything possible to help them feel grounded. Can you see why we give that assignment? It is not just because we are mean old men; it's that each of us has to figure out what that word means.

Shannon McFarland, a student of mine whose life plan is used in the examples in Appendix B, defined success in this way:

Success is earning a comfortable life for yourself and your family. Success is waking up in the morning next to your husband, getting out of bed to make your children's lunches, giving your husband a kiss goodbye as you take the kids to school and head off to work.

Success is family. I will work for my family.

A definition of *success* that I think is very helpful is aligning the goals you seek and the process to get them with your *values*. From that definition, the next step is to realize that you need to clarify your values in terms of both process and outcome.

> **KEYWORD:** Success is living in a way that aligns the goals you seek and the process to get them with your values. As mentioned in Chapter 9, success includes having a career that aligns who you are and what you value with the best benefits the market has to offer. Values are things, both in terms of how you live and the outcomes of your life, that you hold dear.

In the book *The Nature of Human Values* (Free Press, 1973), author Milton Rokeach identified the most common outcome and process values. Table 13.1 lists these values. Outcome values are your ideals or the goals that you strive for. Process values are traits you admire in others and try to cultivate in yourself. Can you pick your top three to five values from each list?

Table 13.1 Values

Outcome values	Process values
A prosperous life	Ambition
An exciting life	Broadmindedness
A sense of accomplishment	Competence
A world at peace	Joy
A world of beauty	Cleanliness
Equality	Courage
Family security	Forgiveness
Freedom	Helpfulness
Happiness	Honesty
Inner harmony	Imagination
Mature love	Independence
National security	Intelligence
Pleasure	Logic
Salvation	Love
Self-respect	Duty
Social recognition	Politeness
True friendship	Responsibility
Wisdom	Self-control

Take a few minutes and think about what is important to you, what matters to you, and what you value most. Then take a sheet of paper and write down why these values matter to you. Write down everything that comes to mind. Put that aside for a day, and then go back and see if you can condense it down to a paragraph or less on what really matters to you.

When I did this, I whittled mine down to one sentence: I want to work with people who want to work toward personal and professional growth. I have devoted my entire career to that. Can you see why a career in auditing was so wrong for me? And why teaching, consulting, and writing are so right for me? What career is right for you?

When you finish Part II of the MAP for Life, you should have the following:

- A written description of what your top process and outcome values are and why those values are so important to you
- A personal definition of success using your values as the foundation
- An ideal person to give you feedback, support, and advice on this part of your plan

At this point, you have two tremendously helpful tools to assess a job offer, whether it comes from your family or from an outside source. Does the offer align with who you are and what you value? Will it move you toward your definition of success?

Part III: The Eight Challenges

You can go back and review the eight challenges if you need to, but first see whether you can fill in the grid in Table 13.2. For each challenge, indicate your estimated level of risk. After you have estimated your risk for each of the eight challenges, choose three that you would like to improve on now.

Table 13.2 Risk Level of Challenges

Challenge	No Risk	Low Risk	Medium Risk	High Risk	Top Three
1. Improving Applied Intelligence					
2. Handling wealth and power					
3. Earning credibility					
4. Writing your own script					
5. Planning your career					
6. Including the family business in your education					
7. Gaining marketability					
8. Getting objective feedback					

To complete this section, you need to do the following:

1. Look at both your personality type and how it relates to the eight challenges by filling out the assessment grid in Table 13.2.
2. List the top three challenges that you want to address in the next six months.
3. Set goals for each challenge.
4. Establish benchmarks to show you that you are making progress with each challenge.
5. Determine the ideal person to give you feedback, support, and advice on this part of your plan.

You may want to look at Appendix B to see how my student addressed these challenges.

Part IV: Career Analysis

In Part IV of the MAP for Life, you address some concrete career issues by completing these tasks:

1. Select one or two careers to consider. If one job is in your family business, I strongly recommend you consider another job, too.
2. Do the internal analysis by looking at how well this career aligns with your personality type, including your strengths and weaknesses, your values, and your definition of success.
3. Do the external analysis by looking at whether you have the skills, credentials, and experiences to get your ideal job. If you don't have these things, set goals for how you will gain them, including benchmarks for those goals.
4. Determine who is the ideal person to give you feedback, support, and advice on this part of your plan.

The Internal Analysis

When I talk about values, most people can't get too much past hard work and honesty. You have to dig deeper in order to find a more specific set of values that you can use to direct your career search and your life. For example, you might value a life filled with accomplishment and great courage, but I might value a life of inner harmony and loving relationships. These different sets of values are equally valid. Your goal should be to align your process and outcome values with your career and your life.

Trevor Whitley, one of my students who graduated in the spring of 2006, wrote one of the most impressive, well thought-out life plans I have seen in the last decade. His father got him interested in the Family Business program (see the Foreword for Trevor's and his father's comments on the program). His 50-page life plan balanced real and honest self-reflection with rigorous research. Trevor completed his life plan as a sophomore and went on to graduate with the first class of those graduating with a major in family business. He had dual majors; the other was in finance.

Though his father is a partner in an accounting firm, Trevor knew he wanted to start outside the family business. He was innovative enough to say he wanted to specialize in advising wealthy families. Along with numerous other impressive accomplishments, Trevor's hard work and planning allowed him to do two internships that aligned with this path and to become the first student on the Family Business Center Board of Advisors, a board that included some members of some of the most prominent family businesses in Florida. By graduation, three firms were interested in him and fascinated by his ability to articulate his values and goals, his plans (which aligned so strongly with the job at hand), and his unique set of qualifications. After all, no one else in the country had this dual major.

One of the most impressive things about Trevor's life plan and my many discussions with him is not merely his career success—although that is impressive. Rather, it is how he defines success as inner harmony. He crafted a very personal and authentic definition of success that was based on an internal value, not an external measurement.

Shannon McFarland, whose plan I include in Appendix B, had the same sense of rigorous research coupled with honest self-analysis. Her life plan was over 60 pages! Now it is not just the number of pages that is impressive (trust me after almost two decades of grading papers, I know that mere page length is not always an accurate measurement of quality), but the fact that all these pages were authentically written.

Remember these key questions you need to answer when doing an internal analysis of a career:

- Does this career path align with who I am?
- Does this career path align with my values?

The Problem with Career Tests

Many career tests list careers that the person who took the test should choose. In other words, the test gives the person a conclusion. When people talk to me about their career test results, they are at best happy that the test has validated a career they have considered. More often, however, people seem frustrated or confused because somehow the listed career choices don't click.

Continued

Continued

I think those tests are convenient because they don't require much work, reflection, or ownership. But that is also their weakness. Because you aren't very involved in the struggle and the process, you don't feel very connected to the outcome. You don't see why the test's conclusion that you should be a plumber in Deland, Florida, fits you.

That's why so much of this book focuses on how to figure out who you are and what you value and how to develop the skills to determine whether a career is right for you. Much of the value is in the journey. I see many students change majors and even career paths once they take the time to clarify who they are and what they want. It's like that old saying, "Give a man a fish and he eats for a day; teach him how to fish, and he'll eat forever." I won't tell you what career to choose; I'll just explain the process you must go through to evaluate your career choices.

External Analysis

In this part of the MAP for Life, you can check out assumptions about your future. Doing a little research before you commit to a career path can save you a lot of unnecessary suffering. Resources on campus, including Career Services, are designed to help with processes like this.

I had a student who thought she might go to pharmacy school, which requires years of additional schooling and hard work. She thought that career made sense given her values and self-assessment. I suggested that she spend a few hours shadowing a pharmacist to see what pharmacists really do before she committed to a program of study.

Job shadowing is going to work with someone doing the job you want to do. It is often for a day, but it can be longer or shorter in duration. After shadowing the pharmacist for a day, my student returned and said she was now certain she did not want to be a pharmacist. Not a bad use of time, was it? A few hours today can save you years of work and tens of thousands of dollars in education costs.

People often choose careers before knowing what the career entails. I often see students who want to be sports lawyers because they love sports or environmental lawyers because they love being outside. However, environmental lawyers often defend the polluters, and most spend very little time outside. Likewise, sports attorneys spend more time in offices than in stadiums. Spending even half a day with someone doing what you think you want to do and checking out your assumptions can forestall a terrible career choice.

The biggest questions to address in this part of the Life Plan are the following:

- What are the skills, credentials, and experiences I need to get this job?
- How do I move from where I am now to being the best person for this job?
- Can I sample the job and see if I would like it on a daily basis?
- What are the key benchmarks that will tell me I am making progress toward being prepared for this job?
- Who can offer me the best feedback, support, and advice for this work?

After determining that her family's values and the values of their business were congruent with her own, Shannon decided on a career in the family firm. However, there were still issues of feedback, credibility, and career development. She set benchmarks for herself, so that she could later evaluate her progress:

My first benchmark is training. The company training program ranks the designers that come out of the program; it is my goal to rank in the Top 3.

Second: First Year Salary. The average first year salary is around $31,000; my goal is $35,000.

Third: Commission Rate. As your sales increase, your commission rate increases. Once you have reached over $90,000 in sales, your commission is bumped up from 7 percent to 9 percent. It is my goal to be in the 9 percent bracket by my fifth month and then to hold it consistently.

Fourth: To gain the credibility and trust from fellow employees through hard work and dedication, not my name. I would like to be promoted to the project manager position, but only if all fellow employees believe that I have earned it as well.

Fifth: To open a second store by the time I am 30.

Credibility, Marketability, and the MAP for Life

The core ideas of credibility and marketability run through all the chapters in this book. Remember, credibility is legitimate self-confidence that you feel and that others can validate. How much more self-confident do you think Trevor, Shannon, or my other students were after completing a 30- to 50- or even 60- page life plan? How much more confident will you be? That self-confidence will be validated by others.

Some very impressive speakers have come to the Stetson University campus from some of the biggest and most prestigious family business in the world. They have been impressed, my clients have been impressed (they have even asked to work with me on their own life plans), and virtually every parent of students in the program since it began in 1998 has been impressed with the MAP for Life results.

Completing the MAP for Life also will enhance your marketability. Marketability is having the skills, credentials, and experiences to develop a career that aligns with your values. The MAP for Life will help with that by giving you the chance to get clear on who you are and what you want. Few people go through this self-assessment, and almost no one builds on that with a values-based definition of success. To align those two with a career choice is rare and very powerful.

If, in a job interview, you can tell the person who might hire you about this plan, then tell them how the job fits into your personality, values, and goals, you will blow away the competition. You will be far more likely to get the job and excel at that career because it will be aligned with what you want.

Conclusion

Planning is a valuable tool for anyone, including people in family businesses. People who have emotional resistance to planning can always create excuses for not planning. However, if you want to take ownership for your life, improve your chances of success, and live an authentic life, planning is a necessary skill.

The MAP for Life's purpose is to help you create a framework to assess any career or career decision and to manage change and transitions in your life. It is not intended to provide you with one unchanging career path that locks you in for the rest of your life. It is the servant, not the master. The four parts of the MAP for Life include a self-assessment using the MBTI, a values-based personal definition of success, an assessment of the most relevant of the eight challenges for you, and a two-part analysis of a career.

Seek out support and resources to help you in your quest to develop your own life plan. This is a professional level challenge, and even professionals have a group to help them. Enlist friends, family, and mentors for the support you need. In the end, however, you alone are responsible for your future. As Sean Connery said to Kevin Costner in *The Untouchables*, "What are you prepared to do?"

I hope that this chapter has helped you to know what you want, move toward it, and get the marketplace to reward you. Remember these key points:

- The MAP for Life is a tool to help you get what you value in a way you can also value.
- Parts I and II of the MAP for Life, the self-assessment and values-based definition of success, remain relatively unchanged throughout a person's life.
- Parts I and II give you the rudder to steer through both the predictable transitions and unexpected changes in life.
- Creating a life plan on your own is a big task, so get all the help you can. Seek support, advice, and feedback from trusted people.

CHAPTER 14

Creating Your Portfolio

If you have read and worked on everything in this book up to this point, you are ready for the last step: showing the world you are a professional. You can demonstrate that you have done a great deal of introspection, hard work, and planning and are now ready to offer the benefits of that preparation to the marketplace, be it in your family's business or elsewhere.

How do you package and present your work, which so far has been for your benefit, and transform it into something that demonstrates to a company that you are a professional? You create a portfolio. Your portfolio will enable you to present your skills, credentials, and experiences, and thus give you the best chance possible to get your ideal job and ultimately achieve great success in life.

By the end of this chapter, you will

- Know the purpose of a portfolio.
- Connect your life plan to your portfolio.
- Be able to use the portfolio to demonstrate your skills, credentials, and experiences.
- Maintain your portfolio as your career progresses.
- Seek feedback on your portfolio.

Understanding the Purpose of a Portfolio

The *portfolio* should demonstrate your skills, credentials, and experiences. It shows the organization that is considering hiring you information that demonstrates your abilities. Whereas your life plan demonstrates credibility, your portfolio needs to demonstrate your *marketability*.

> **KEYWORD:** A **portfolio** is the material that supports your resume and gives the marketplace evidence of the skills, credentials, and experiences you have for a given career path. It packages and presents your marketability. **Marketability** means having the skills, credentials, and experiences to get a job that aligns with your values. It is the external aspects of the credibility you worked on in your life plan. To truly be marketable, you must earn at least one job offer that is from a business not owned by your family.

Less directly, your portfolio should also demonstrate that you are someone whom people get along with and that you are socially intelligent. With your portfolio, do you create a reputation as a professional, as someone who can graciously acknowledge how much others have helped you, and as a person who is willing to learn? Your portfolio should convey your character as well as your accomplishments.

When I meet with a client, especially for the first meeting, I always try to keep this thought in mind, "Give them a sample; don't try to sell them." A resume is a jumping-off point to sell yourself, but a portfolio is more of a sample of your work. In a portfolio, you gather proof of the work you have done and credentials you have earned into one binder to put in front of the person who is thinking about hiring you.

Before you begin compiling your portfolio, complete the internal and external analysis of the career path you have chosen and get a description of the job you are considering. A typical portfolio contains the following items:

- Personal statement
- Resume
- Letters of recommendation
- Work samples and other supporting materials

The following sections explain each of these items in more detail.

Personal Statement

Write a personal statement related to how this position fulfills your personal definition of success. In this context, your focus should be more on the professional aspects of your vision of success. In a paragraph or so, but no more than a page, tell the employer why this position is so well aligned with what you want out of life.

This statement shows that you are likely to be both a satisfied and committed member of the team because the job corresponds with your goals for your life. Writing this statement will also help you prepare for the interview and show how you are not just a qualified applicant, but a great fit for the company as well.

My former student Trevor Whitley framed his portfolio in terms of his definition of success, both in business and his personal life. This statement sums up his overall objective:

> *Success for me translates into living out my instrumental goals in order to attain the first four of my outcome-based values, and hopefully receive validation in my fifth process-based value. My process values are honesty, forgiveness, love, helpfulness, and intelligence. My outcome values are salvation, inner harmony, wisdom, happiness, and social recognition.*

Trevor expanded his personal mission statement into his career objectives, including his desire to earn according to his market value and other overall career factors, including his personal values:

For me, success begins with my value for inner harmony. I seek a job that pays a salary comparable to my market value ... A further measurement of success is my happiness with my job, coworkers, and the city in which I am living. Finally, I seek employment with a company known for its "corporate culture" in the areas of integrity, honesty, and customer service... [T]his desire for corporate integrity is essential to my development of inner harmony.

How I will determine success in my life and career is through the next three [values]: inner harmony, wisdom, and happiness. Inner harmony is the key struggle here. I will judge my life and career based upon whether I am inherently happy with what I do...My level of contentedness, satisfaction, and/or happiness in each individual area of my life will lead to inner harmony. I think that if one or more of these areas is out of whack, it would be a detriment to my inner satisfaction.

Wisdom for me is acting with integrity and honor, in a mature manner. Making the wise choice is not always, or even normally, the easiest path, but I have found that when I choose the easy way out, it sets off my inner harmony. Happiness, or contentedness, is much the same as inner harmony. It may just be the outward expression of that inner harmony. I would say that honesty and wisdom is following my gut or intuition in making the hard decisions in life, rather than following anybody else's scripts.

How can this be validated beyond me? That comes in my fifth outcome-based value: social recognition. I do not think it is absolutely necessary in the same way as the other four, but it would be the ultimate validation of credibility – either through my professional career or community activities. There is definitely a tension here between inner harmony and external validation. Obviously achieving both is the goal, but I am comfortable saying that inner harmony is priority number one. I am able to overcome not being externally validated if I am satisfied with myself. But if I achieve external validation without inner harmony, that would be an empty validation.

He then narrows down his career objectives to specifics:

I am seeking a company that will allow me to grow in my job. While I understand that the nature of the financial advising business requires experience to gain the trust of employees, you have to be given the opportunity to gain that experience. As I demonstrate my capabilities, I would ask for my responsibilities to be extended, allowing me to grow into the role of advisor to clients.

I am also seeking a company that is willing to mentor me in this process. Success at the end of five years would be the attainment of both CFA and CFP [Chartered Financial Analyst and Certified Financial Planner] distinctions and a promotion or other job offer in a full advising position. Any company that I join must be willing to support me in seeking both CFA and CFP designations within the first five years, after which I will evaluate the pros and cons of an MBA [Master of Business Administration].

Finally, success in my job would be having the autonomy to directly advise clients within the first five years. My ideal company would also support community activities in which I am involved (religious, philanthropic, sports-related, etc.). I am willing to trade off a higher salary and possibly more rapid advancement in order to have free time to pursue these interests.

My Perspective on Resumes

From my perspective as a consultant, professor, and employer, I believe you should view employers as organizations that are facing problems. As such, they want to hire someone who can solve their problems. Think of it as though they have a fire in a room down the hall and they want to have it put out. There are only two real questions: Can you put out their fire? And if so, will you fit in with the other employees? The portfolio answers that first question; it shows them you can put out the fire.

I think most people, especially students, make the mistake of wanting their resumes to tell their life story. That's okay, I suppose, if you're selling your life story. However, your prospective employers aren't looking for a good story—they're looking for someone to put out fires. They also probably have between 100 and 1,000 resumes, so you should focus on making sure your resume clearly states how you will solve their problems. Make it easy for them to connect the dots, and your resume will stand out.

So how do you make sure they see you are the person best suited to put out their fire? Conceptually, you first take the job description that lists the skills (firefighting), credentials (degree in firefighting), and experiences (put out five fires at my last job) with which you want to align yourself. Make certain your resume is structured to specifically align with the job listing. That makes the reviewer's job easier by making the connection no one else is going to take the time to make. If you do this advance work, it will enable the reviewer to quickly and clearly see how you can solve the organization's problems.

Think about it. Companies have created want ads or job descriptions, which are their profiles of their ideal candidate, the person they think they need to solve their problems. The first impression of you a firm gets comes from your resume. Therefore, your resume should build a bridge between you and the company's image of the ideal candidate.

Your portfolio supports the claims you make in your resume. It is the proof that you have the skills, credentials, and experiences that your resume lists. It might include an evaluation from your supervisor of your firefighting skills and the special skills you have learned, such as how to use the latest technology in firefighting equipment. For credentials you can show degrees, continuing education, or awards you have earned and even why the institution that granted it is noteworthy. Perhaps it is "the top ranked program in office firefighting four years in a row in *BusinessWeek's* annual ranking," for example.

Although detailed resume advice is beyond the scope of this book, there are books, courses, and other resources to help you to create the best resume possible. Use them. Start by checking out the following Web sites:

JIST Publishing: www.jist.com

Princeton Review: www.princetonreview.com

Monster: www.resume.monster.com

Career Builder: www.careerbuilder.com

Recommendation Letters and Other Supporting Materials

Though there is a growing trend for business students to use portfolios, other fields have traditionally used them. Artists, models, and engineers often use portfolios of their work. An artist can show the art she has completed or shown at art galleries. The model can show commercials, fashion shows, promotions, and other work he has done. An engineer might show projects in which she was involved, testimony from satisfied clients, and related material. The supporting materials you include will vary according to your field of interest, your experience, and your training, but generally you will want to include samples of your work, additional feedback or acknowledgement from others, and materials that show your depth of experience.

Your portfolio also should include at least one letter of recommendation (ideally two) from a past employer or teacher. These letters should talk about your character, but also comment on your skills, credentials, and experiences to the extent they are relevant. Help your employers or teachers link their letters to the job description if possible.

Linking Your Life Plan and Your Portfolio

You do the MAP for Life for yourself. It is personal, and it may be something you share with only one other person. Its focus is to help you increase your credibility. You will feel much more self-confident after all that self-assessment, values clarification, and reflection on which of the eight challenges you need to address.

When you create a life plan, you go through a profoundly important process. In Part IV of the MAP for Life, you analyze a career from the internal aspects, and then you analyze it in terms of the external aspects: the skills, credentials, and experiences you will need. Going through that process develops skills that will help you manage career change for the rest of your life.

Your life plan lays the groundwork for the only authentic path to success, which is to be marketable in a career path that aligns with your personality and values. The goal of the portfolio is to take all that is relevant from your work on the life plan and package it to show a prospective employer, whether your family's business or any other business, how great you'd be at putting out its fires. Imagine how few people who are applying for this job have done the work that you have.

Trevor wanted to build on the success of his life plan. He wanted to be able to demonstrate to employers that he had the skills, credentials, and experiences to deserve a career with a firm that gave financial advice to wealthy families, and he wanted his portfolio to demonstrate his marketability. When he created his portfolio, Trevor linked his resume to his life plan with a personal statement that began with his own definition of success, and then linked that to his chosen career and his values.

Of course, you need more than a good set of values. You also need to be qualified for the job. If the position requires 20 years experience as a CEO and you are 22, all this work and a great portfolio still won't get you the job. Let's assume you are qualified. You are also in that 3 to 5 percent of people who have any written life goals, and all this additional work probably puts you in the top 1 percent as far as written life goals go. As an employer, I would be impressed. That sense of proactiveness, self-awareness, and ownership for your life would make you look like a professional.

Remember these key points about the MAP for Life and your portfolio:

- The MAP for Life is internal. It is for you and focuses on your credibility.
- The MAP for Life lays the foundation for your portfolio.
- Parts I and II of the MAP for Life don't change very often, but Parts III and IV of the MAP for Life and your portfolio will change more often.

- Your portfolio is more external. Design it to show prospective employers and demonstrate your marketability.
- Your life plan and your portfolio show you have earned the right to be a professional in the top 1 percent of people in setting life goals.

Presenting Your Skills, Credentials, and Experiences

What might your portfolio look like? When you are thinking about how to organize your information, keep in mind that you need to connect the dots for the prospective employer. You can list your skills on your resume and then use samples of your work to demonstrate that you have these skills. These examples concretely demonstrate to employers that you can do what the job requires, and they get to see it, not just read a line on a resume. You also should link your credentials and experiences to the current prospective job as directly as possible.

Trevor was able to show the skills he had developed, from financial skills like analyzing a client's financial situation to family business skills like summarizing a family history. Building on that, he was able to show assignments he had done, including samples of his work from both the financial side and the family business side. He had letters of recommendation, awards, and academic honors. All these items showed how qualified he was. The following sections provide more information about how to present your skills, credentials, and experiences.

Skills

In your portfolio, list each skill you see in the job description and consider writing a paragraph that creates a bridge or link between the job description, your resume, and the supporting material. At the end of each paragraph, you can instruct the reader to look at the work samples you have included in the portfolio for further information about your skill level.

Samples of your work are often a great way to demonstrate you have the skills the employer wants. If your work was graded or evaluated by a teacher or employer and received positive feedback, include it as well. You should also include awards or acknowledgments show that you have earned or been recognized for a certain skill level.

In his portfolio, Trevor listed his people skills, information skills, and skills with objects, and then organized them for presentation into those relating to finance and family business, the two main career areas on which he wanted to focus. To demonstrate these skills, he also included a stock research report and a bond research report that he had created for the Roland George Program. These reports showed that he could analyze and value a common stock or a bond.

Finance Related

In-depth analysis of financial statements

Evaluation of companies for stock or bond investments

Evaluation of mutual funds for investment

Valuation of commercial real estate properties

Evaluation of a client's risk tolerance and appropriate asset allocations

Creation of customized comprehensive financial plans

Family Business Related

Analyzing the three systems embedded in families that own businesses

Constructing a family genogram to deduce trends

Applying the process consulting approach in addition to expert advising

Dealing with emotional resistance in a client or client system and facilitating breakthroughs

Developing succession plans that fit the client's values

Facilitating the transfer of wealth between generations

Credentials

What are the necessary or important credentials for (promotion in) this job? Examples of credentials include certification, licensure, or degrees. Your portfolio should show that you have all the necessary credentials for the job you want.

Make certain that you clearly explain to the reader how the credentials you include demonstrate your abilities. For example, "the Smith family scholarship shows I have a strong sense of civic mindedness because each year over two hundred students apply and must demonstrate their civic involvement, and I was chosen above all others."

Trevor focused on finance- and family business-related accomplishments when listing his credentials:

Finance Related

2005 Financial Executives Institute Distinguished Student Award, Central Florida chapter

NASD Series 65 certification

CFA Level 1 candidate (pending June 3 test)

Academic year 2005-2006 Roland George Investments Institute student trustee

Fall 2005 Roland George merit scholar

Family Business Related

One of only five family business majors in the country (first class of graduates from the only major program in the country)

2005 USA-Today All College Academic Team nominee

2004 Family Business merit scholar

Author of 50-page life development plan

Experiences

What are the experiences you have had that demonstrate that you have the skills, credentials, and leadership you claim? Here is where you can leverage your credibility by saying how impressive your school, your employer, or your volunteer organization is. (For example, "I worked with the largest relief organization in the nation on a hurricane relief team to bring supplies to New Orleans aid workers.")

State the amount of time you spent with an organization and work you completed. One project in a class is good, but 20 projects in your part-time job over the last five years are better. If it helps and is relevant, write in your portfolio how this work affected the organization.

In Trevor Whitley's portfolio, he listed concrete examples of experiences that demonstrated he had the skills and leadership ability for his chosen career, specializing in financial consulting to family businesses:

EXPERIENCE

Finance Related

Investments & Trust Administration Intern, [a private wealth investment company], summer 2003

Financial Planning Intern, MNS Financial Management, summers 2004 and 2005

Stetson University Roland George Investments Institute, 2005-2006

Family Business Related

Family Office Intern, Root Company, fall 2004

Stetson University Family Business Center Board of Advisors, 2003-2006

Stetson University Family Business Center Student Ambassador

Make sure to frame or position your credentials and experiences in the most favorable light possible. You can enhance your credibility with the credibility of places in which you gained experience and organizations where you earned your credentials.

In Trevor's case, he graduated with majors in both family business and finance. In his portfolio, he had to be able to explain to companies not only what a major in family business is, but also how it could help him better serve their clients. Note how he highlighted his college career experiences, legitimately framing their uniqueness and importance:

Throughout my university experience, I have aspired to be an ethical and innovative leader in both the classroom and my cocurricular activities. In a sense, my greatest intellectual endeavor is not one thing, but the culmination of my involvement in Stetson University's Family Business Center. The Center is the nation's leading academic program devoted to the next generation of family business leaders. As the first person in the nation to graduate with a major in Family Business, I have had the unique experience of working closely with the faculty to customize my education and create for myself a unique opportunity for future benefit to society.

Research at Stetson University has indicated that 42 percent of business majors come from families that own businesses. Beyond that, family businesses account for 80 to 90 percent of all business in the country and create approximately 78 percent of all new jobs. Unfortunately, only about one-third of these businesses will survive past the first generation, and nobody is talking about the unique situation facing these businesses: that of managing the overlap of the family and the business. No other university in the country offers students any discussion on if, when, how, and why to join their family's business. As a major in Family Business, I have approximately 600-800 hours of such training.

I consider my 2004 award in Family Business as the start of this endeavor. I have established myself in the classroom as an outstanding student through the creation of a 50-page life plan and was invited by the Director to represent family business students as a member of the Center's Board of Advisors. Since that time, I have applied my knowledge in an internship, and as a member of the board, I have helped to further develop the curriculum and set the strategic direction of the Family Business Center. Additionally, I have been recognized by the director as the best student in this innovative program for three years running. All together, my work in this field of study has positioned me with the knowledge, skills, and desire to offer society what no other student in the country can offer.

Family business is a vitally important and underserved institution of our society and is integral to our nation's future economic stability. When done properly, I believe that nothing can create more value in society. Families that own businesses tend to have greater clarity of their values and work to integrate them into their business practices. Their businesses have a longer-term focus as well as a tendency to emphasize philanthropy and stewardship. I believe our society and culture will benefit greatly from this type of clarification of values, longer-term focus, and dedication that family businesses provide.

Family and business are two significant cornerstones of our nation's values, and the synthesis of such values drives our economic future. As the first person to graduate from the only family business major in the country, I will be the only person in the country academically qualified to provide the advice needed to guarantee that these businesses will continue to positively impact society in the future. There is no greater need in business today.

Prepare for the Interview

My father once gave me some advice that I share with my students. He told me, "The meeting is over before the meeting begins." That statement might seem very Zen-like, but it means that if you are prepared for a meeting, the desired outcome is far more likely to happen. Be prepared for your interview.

A professional is prepared for an interview by being able to clearly and concisely articulate the direct link from the company's job description to her resume and portfolio. In just two to three minutes, you should be able to verbalize that to the person interviewing you. That is how you make the results of the meeting much more predictable.

Because of his life plan, Trevor was able to clearly articulate in each of the three interviews he lined up how a career advising families of wealth aligned with his values. He could easily explain how such a career would enable him to succeed and what success meant to him personally, which was pretty darned impressive. His work on his portfolio made it easy for him to connect his skills, credentials, and experiences with the needs of the companies he interviewed with. As a result, all three of the firms he interviewed with showed interest in him.

Establishing Marketability with a Portfolio

Now you know that our old friend, Tony the amateur, would say, "Yeah, but if I am interviewing with my family business, I don't have to write a resume and create a portfolio. They know me already." That's true. Your parents and the rest of your family know you as a family member. However, they probably don't know you as a professional, but they should.

Besides, why would you ever give your family less opportunity to see your worth than you would give a stranger? If you are interviewing with your family business, whether with a family member, nonfamily member, or both, you should see this as a wonderful opportunity to show them your marketability. Remember, you should never work for your family because you think it is the easier route. If you are committed to establishing your marketability, you need to interview with a firm *besides* your family anyway. Your value in the marketplace is what someone besides your family's business is willing to pay you. You can't get that feedback without getting an interview and an offer.

Credibility and marketability are two sides of the same coin, and that coin buys your success. You need to feel good about your abilities in a legitimate way, a way that others can validate. To build on that credibility, you need the marketplace to value what you do.

Being a member of the next generation, you always need to feel legitimate in your eyes and be perceived as legitimate in the eyes of others. Marketability says that you have this job because you have earned it and you are keeping this job because your performance warrants it. The most devastating thing you can do as a member of the next generation from a family business is to work in your family business and not be credible and marketable. I have talked about the credibility risk in other chapters, especially Chapter 13, but I want to stress that it strongly and directly links to marketability.

If you are working for your family's business and are not qualified or not performing, then you are not being treated as the marketplace would treat you. Thus your credibility and marketability will suffer. You have to protect, cultivate, and improve your marketability. That is perhaps even more applicable to you as a member of a family that owns a business than other people, because you have more risks and temptations to navigate.

Along this line of thinking, realize that if you work in your family business that you need to be very mindful of having a good resume. Why would you have a resume and portfolio for your family business that wasn't as least as professional as you would for another business?

Updating Your Portfolio

From time to time, you will need to update your portfolio. First, you will need to tailor it to each job you apply for. However, this may require only very small changes, unless the jobs are very different. One of my students had a master file and varied it depending on the job. I recommend that you consider doing that.

You also will update your portfolio as you rack up greater accomplishments. If you attend a week-long leadership program, get an award for being the top salesperson, or accept the nomination to head the board of your professional association, you should add these accomplishments to your portfolio file. This maintenance requires some work, but it will also boost your self-esteem. As I jokingly said to some close friends when I put together material for a job interview, "If I didn't know me so well, I would be impressed!" This process allows you to step back and appreciate all that you have accomplished.

Getting Feedback

A job search is an exciting time, but it can be stressful. Especially if you have not been through a search for your first professional position, take your time and do it right. Advice on job searches is beyond the scope of this book, but all eight challenges come into play here. If you have dealt with them, they can add to your chances of success. If you haven't, they can diminish your chances.

Take a few minutes and consider who can help you and how. Can your friends give you a pep talk? Can your family be supportive? Is there a professor, perhaps the one that wrote you a letter of recommendation, who can help you choose work samples for your portfolio? Can a person in a management position (family is okay, beyond family is better) assist your with your interviewing skills? Ask someone you know and trust for feedback on your resume, your portfolio, and your job search. If you are in college, you might ask if the career services folks on your campus can help you. You can ask your guidance counselor for help if you are in high school or a career coach if you have graduated.

We all have strong areas and areas where we need support. For some folks, networking might be a strength, but completing tasks without a deadline might be a weakness. For others, the opposite might be true. Take ownership of your strong suits and shortfalls, and ask for help when you need it. Remember that your professional development is a lifelong process.

Conclusion

You have a great deal to offer, and you deserve to package and present that to all the firms that interest you, including your family's firm. I hope you will strive to translate your hard work into a format that empowers you.

As you create your portfolio, think about these main points from this chapter:

- With a portfolio, you can link an employer's job description to your resume by providing samples of your work.
- The portfolio includes the aspects of your life plan that you want to share with the world.
- Your portfolio should be tailored to a specific job and show that you already have the skills, credentials, and experiences to do the job.
- Help from books, the Career Services department on campus, mentors, professors, friends, and family can motivate you in your job search and can guide you toward your goal of personal and professional success.

If you have done the work and applied the concepts covered in this book, you have now increased your chances to 80 percent or more that you will find a sustainable career path that aligns with your values and reduced to less than 20 percent the risk of derailing your career, just by understanding and meeting the eight challenges. Now comes the ultimate challenge. By working through this book, you have acquired the best-equipped toolbox available. Now all you need to do is put those tools to good use—to apply them to the raw materials at hand and build the career, and the future, of your dreams.

I believe in you. Now all you need to do is believe in yourself. Good luck!

APPENDIX A

Additional Resources

Online Sources

Center for Applications of Psychological Type
www.capt.org

Center for Creative Leadership
www.ccl.org

Family Firm Institute
www.ffi.org

Human Metrics (for free Jung/MBTI Type Assessment)
www.humanmetrics.com

GenoPro (for genogram information and software)
www.genopro.com/genogram

McCann & Associates
www.gregmccannspeaks.com
www.familybusinesshelp.com
www.mccannfbconsulting.com

The Princeton Review
www.princetonreview.com/cte

Books on Personality Type

Enhancing Leadership Effectiveness by Roger Pearman

Families: Using Type to Enhance Mutual Understanding by Charles Ginn

In the Grip by Naomi Quenk

Introduction to Type in Organizations by Sandra Hirsh and Jean Kummerow

Looking at Type: The Fundamentals by Charles Martin

Meeting the Shadow by Connie Zweig and Jeremiah Abrams

Procrastination by Judith Provost

Type Talk by Otto Kroeger and Janet Thuesen

Books on Self-Improvement

Do What You Are by Paul D. Tieger and Barbara Barron-Tieger

Now, Discover Your Strengths by Marcus Buckingham and Donald Clifton

Ongoing Feedback by Kirkland and Manoogian (available at www.ccl.org)

Please Understand Me: Character and Temperament Types by David Keirsey and Marilyn Bates

What Color Is Your Parachute? by Richard Nelson Bolles

Books on Family Business

Family Wealth, Keeping It in the Family by James Hughes

Managing for the Long Run by Danny Miller and Isabelle LeBreton-Miller

Working with the Ones You Love by Dennis Jaffe

Working with Family Businesses by David Bork, etc.

The Seasons of a Man's Life by Daniel Levinson

The Daughter Also Rises by Anne Francis

Wealthy & Wise (secrets about money) edited by Heidi Steiger, Neuberger Berman

The Survival Guide for Business Families by Gerald Le Van

Getting Along in Family Business by Edwin Hoover and Colette Lombard Hoover

The McCann Action Plan for Life Outline

The McCann Action Plan (MAP) for Life is a project you should work on over a period of time. The purpose of this plan is to help you analyze who you are, what you value, how you define success, and what all of this means for your future in terms of your career. This plan works best when it is part of an ongoing process. In its broadest sense, the MAP for Life enables you to take ownership for your life and be more proactive.

I have included examples from a life plan by a former student, Shannon McFarland. Shannon had the opportunity to go into her family's furniture business after graduation. She ultimately did so. However, the decision to enter the family firm came after lengthy introspection and much consideration of the challenges inherent in that decision. You will see from the examples that creating the life plan gave Shannon a lot of insight into her family's dynamic. She put a lot of work into figuring out whether she should take a job in the family business, as well as how to improve her chances of success once there.

The MAP for Life

I. Self-Assessment, Family, and Family Business
A. Who are you?

Self-understanding is the key to effective leadership. The lack of it can derail your career as you progress in an organization.

1. Based upon the Myers-Briggs Type Indicator results, how do you prefer to:

   a. Communicate?

   b. Process information?

   c. Make decisions?

   d. Organize your life?

2. How do these preferences relate to such issues as time management, stress, family dynamics, and business leadership?

   Example: Seeing that my father and I are both introverts, I now realize why we usually have the same complaints about my mom and about Joseph (my boyfriend). They are both extraverts. My father and I are both always asking my mother to stop talking!

3. What are the strengths and areas for development for your personality?

   Example: I pride myself on having a good work ethic. I get everything that needs to be done ... done. I take my time and do it the best I can the first time. I hate having to go back and do things because I didn't take the time the first time, which is a waste of my time.

   However, these strengths also hinder me at times. Sometimes I wish I didn't have a strong work ethic or sense of responsibility. Then I could just blow stuff off, go out, and have fun.

   I think most of the improvements I wish to make are linked to self-confidence. I know that I have to work on that before I can work on the other issues.

4. Given your current relationships and position (be it in school or in a job), where can you make your biggest contributions and where can you focus on developing select skills?

5. How does your personality type relate to others in your family and your family's business?

B. What issues affect your self-assessment?

1. Where is your unwillingness to address certain issues holding you back? How does that emotional resistance serve you and how does it not serve you?

   Example: My feeling overwhelmed is usually caused by emotional resistance to doing something. When I get stressed, I tend to put more weight or emphasis on things that I need to get done than there really is. Because of this I feel more of a pressure to get things accomplished correctly than there really is.

   I noticed this with the Sorority of the Year Application. I spent two weeks of my life on that application. I wanted to do it right so that if we didn't win, it wasn't because of who wrote it, it was because of the chapter. However, I had more stressed out moments than normal during that week. I now see that they were due more to the fact that I felt I had to prove myself through this application than the actual application itself.

   When does being emotionally resistant work for me? When I don't have to time to divulge deeper. Or when I am talking to someone I just met or that doesn't know me that well. If someone in the cafeteria came up to me and said, "Hey, I heard you were going to go to UM. What happened?," I am not going to answer, "Oh, well, I am terrified to leave the comfort of my parents, so I stayed close to home."

2. What are some basic issues that relate to all families that could inform your understanding of your role in your family and your family business? Examples include life cycles and the impact of stress on family.

3. What is your role in the family? What is your role in the family business?

   Example: I see myself as really only having one role: I am the daughter. Yes, I work at the family business from time to time, but I mainly work in the office and everyone knows I am the daughter. I will be taking on my second role in January of 2007 when I become a designer in the business. I am very interested to see how this works out with the other designers; as of right now, I have a good relationship with all of them. However, I am a little nervous of actually working alongside them

   In my family interview, I asked both of my parents what they would like me to call them when I am employed in the business. Mom answered, "Mom," and Dad answered, "Dad." Therefore, I don't see there being a real

Continued

differentiation between my two roles. I believe that my mom is more apt to treat me as an employee than my father. My father is the type who would never want to upset me and always wants to make sure that I am taken care of no matter what.

4. What are the defining traditions and patterns in your family (and your family business)?

   Example: Eighty-five percent of the conversation that goes on at our dinner table is about the business. The McFarlands are the business. It is hard to set boundaries at this point in time because I am not really "in" the business full-time yet, and the only way I hear about business-related issues is at home. I know, from the interview, that my father wished there would be boundaries between work and home.

   I think that being an only child has a lot to do with the overlap factor. My parents are always telling me that I can go off and do what I want and what makes me happy, as long as I call them once a day to let them know what I am doing. This does happen; I talk to my mom about two times a day and my dad about once. If my mom and I haven't talked at all in a day, I feel very uncomfortable.

   However, I am able to differentiate when it comes to moods and attitudes. I will always listen to what my mom has to say, but that doesn't mean I blindly follow her, this is true of my father too.

5. What are the values of your family and how do they align or conflict with your personal values?

C. What do you know about the family business?

1. What is the history of the family business (founding, ownership, management, family involvement)?

2. What are the values of the family business?

II. Values

A. What are your core values, both in terms of how you do things and the outcomes you want?

   Example: Success is earning a comfortable life for yourself and your family. Success is waking up in the morning next to your husband, getting out of bed to make your children's lunches, and giving your husband a kiss goodbye as you take the kids to school and head off to work. Success is family. I will work for my family.

B. Can you craft a personal vision of success that aligns with your values?

Imagine that you had to share this personal vision of success with a spouse, a business partner, and a mentor. Is your definition clear enough to enable these three folks to, with reasonable certainty, predict how you might decide on a career decision (such as the one you are dealing with in Part III)?

1. Does your vision of success align with your family's values?

2. How well does your current position align with these values?

3. How well does your role in your family align with these values?

Example: There are many values in our family business. The main value of the business is family. The business is there for the family and has built the family. Perhaps that's why the family is the business.

Some outcome-related values include: a comfortable life, a sense of accomplishment, and social recognition. Some process-related values of the business are to be capable, ambitious, honest, logical, loving, responsible, and harmonious.

The values of the business, the family, and others involved closely with the business are what drive the business. Every decision is made with every employee and family member in mind. I believe that values are very important in such a small business. As one of our noted guest speakers said, "Without values, you can't earn trust; without trust, you can't have commitment." A business is almost impossible to run without commitment.

III. The Eight Challenges

A. Select your top three challenges from this book to work on.

If you can't decide, let me suggest you look at Applied Intelligence, obtaining
feedback, and writing your own script.

1. Practicing Applied Intelligence

Example: I believe self-awareness ties closely into Applied Intelligence. You constantly have to be aware of your attitude and the character that you portray to the outside world. When I was competing for a national baton twirling title, it was brought to my attention by my coach that some competitors and judges saw me as stuck up and snobby. Neither my coach nor I really could understand why; however, that is not a good reputation to have (especially with the judges) when a national title is on the line. To help us figure out how I got this reputation, my coach went to one of her friends

Continued

who was also a judge.

We found out that I was perceived as snobby and stuck up because of my lack of participation with the other contestants. In my mind, I was being focused; I didn't spend a lot of time interacting and chatting with the other contestants because I believed my time was better spent preparing mentally and physically for the competition. So while they were all talking in a circle, I was in the corner focusing on the competition at hand. I believed that I was there for one reason: to compete, not to socialize.

How I was being perceived wasn't in synch with my true character. Therefore, I had to take time out and try really hard at the following competitions to be more social. From then on out, I have always taken the time to step back and ask myself, "How will this decision affect how people see me?"

2. Managing wealth and power

3. Earning credibility

   Example: I hope to gain marketability and credibility through my first years working in the family business. I hope to be able to prove myself in a way. The business is so small that people know what is going on all the time. It would be impossible for me to be getting outside assistance or pay without anyone else knowing about it. That is something that I would never want. I want to work my way up through the business. I don't want to be promoted to project manager until I have earned it. If we open another store, I want my parents to look for outside managers. I will apply as well and let the best qualified person win.

4. Writing your own script

   Example: My parent's plan is for me to work as a design consultant for at least three years. If I would like to stay there longer, then they have already said they would support that. However, if I do well after three years, a project manager position would be my next step. This is a new position to the company and is still in the works at the corporate level; therefore, I am not sure of the pay and benefits.

   My plan: I believe it is a good idea to come into the business as a design consultant in order to understand the product. Our family name is built around the product, and in order to hold any other title or position within the company, you have to know the product inside and out. I also think the consultant's job will be a good way for me to enhance my people skills.

Once I get a feel for the product, which I don't necessarily think will take three years, I hope to move into a management position, like project manager. The project manager position was actually my father's and my idea. When I took the FOCUS questionnaire (an interest and skill assessment) from Career Services, it showed that my strengths were time management, organization, and delegation. Therefore, it follows that I am more suited for a type of management or human resource (because of my psychology background) position. If I were not planning on going into my family business, I would look for jobs in the human resources/management arenas.

As far as the training goes for the interior design position, I had a long talk with both of my parents about this because I didn't feel that it was the best idea for either of them to train me. I decided that I wanted to go to the company's five-week course and then to a leadership training session. I might not attend the training session until I have put in time at the store at home and am looking into management opportunities in our business.

5. Planning your career

6. Including the family business in your college experience

7. Avoiding the golden handcuffs and gaining marketability

8. Obtaining objective feedback

B. Apply the three-point analysis to each of your top challenges.

1. Related to each challenge, address your own emotional resistance to taking full ownership for your attitude and behavior. What defenses are you using? What are the costs (and even benefits) to any patterns you are stuck in? Review Chapter 4 for more help on this issue.

2. How can you involve your family in working on this challenge? Involving your family can mean talking with them and asking them for feedback, support, or advice. It can also mean drawing some boundaries with them about what you want to talk about and when you chose to talk about it. It can also mean seeking feedback, support, or advice from people beyond your family. One of the signs that you are individuating is when you broaden your network and rely more on peers and nonfamily mentors.

3. Given your enhanced awareness of yourself and your personality, do

Continued

you realize where you are not effectively conveying your true character and thus putting your reputation at risk? Can you get feedback on this? Remember that initially most of us think we have little room for improvement in this area. If that is how you feel, be patient and open-minded and dig a little deeper.

IV. Career

Note: This section needs to be tailored to the career choice or life decision at hand. The overriding theme is to address the decision from two perspectives: internal and external.

A. Internal

1. How well does this new position align with both your process and outcome values?

2. How does the years of research on your personality from the Myers-Briggs type inform your decision?

3. Does this decision move you closer to your definition of success in terms of both process and outcome?

B. External

1. What career or career decision are you considering?

2. What are the job requirements (skills, credentials, and experiences) for this career?

3. What is the offer (job title and salary) from your family business? From the marketplace? How does this compare to others with similar credentials? Analyze any difference.

   Example: The offer from my family business is nothing grand. Both of my parents believe that I should start at the bottom, or at least the bottom for women in the business (you don't find many women if any working in the warehouse). I am being offered the design consultant position. This position … only really requires an associate's degree (sometimes no degree is necessary). Therefore, I am not being offered anything above what I am qualified for. The average first year salary is around $31,000. The design consultant position is based strictly on commission, and I will not be earning anything above and beyond the commission rates of other designers.

4. What are the skills, credentials, and experiences you need to obtain this career (and how/when will you get them)?

5. What are the benchmarks needed to assess your progress?

Example: My first benchmark is training. The company training program ranks the designers that come out of the program; it is my goal to rank in the Top 3.

Second: First Year Salary. The average first year salary is around $31,000; my goal is $35,000.

Third: Commission Rate. As your sales increase, your commission rate increases. Once you have reached over $90,000 in sales, your commission is bumped up from 7 percent to 9 percent. It is my goal to be in the 9 percent bracket by my fifth month and then to hold it consistently.

Fourth: To gain the credibility and trust from fellow employees through hard work and dedication, not my name. I would like to be promoted to the project manager position, but only if all fellow employees believe that I have earned it as well.
Fifth: To open a second store by the time I am 30.

6. Who can give you objective feedback? Consider someone beyond family and friends.

Example: I don't really have anyone who can give me honest feedback. The closest I have to that is my coach, but even overall I don't think she would be completely honest with me if it was something that she thought would really hurt me. So, I don't know where to turn to for complete and honest feedback. I don't even know where to look.

Here was my thought process on the subject. My parents? No, they are way too biased. My grandparents? No, for the same reason. The manager at the store is too close to my parents. The designers already lie to me all the time because they work for my parents.

I have mentioned before that I am not sure where I will be able to get real objective feedback. I am hoping that my fellow employees will eventually be able to give me objective feedback. Also, I am hoping that the office manager will be able to give me objective feedback as well. However, I think this may take time and considerable effort to make him feel comfortable enough to be able to give me true objective feedback.

7. What outside research would help? Would you consider two hours on this if it would help?

Continued

8. Given your academic credentials, career experience, and skills, what is a reasonable salary?

9. What can your family or a mentor do to help?

10. How does your personality type fit in?

11. How will this transition enhance your credibility and marketability?

ABOUT THE AUTHOR

Greg McCann, JD is the award-winning founder and director of Stetson University's internationally prominent Family Enterprise Center. He has also worked with numerous universities in the U.S., Europe, and Australia to help them develop their family business programs.

As both a full professor of business and founder of McCann & Associates family business consulting firm, McCann helps family enterprises with succession planning, developing the next generation, and other issues. He is a Family Firm Institute fellow and was a member of their board of directors, an international organization dedicated to helping family business advisors, educators, and researchers and to increasing awareness of the field.

McCann has received the Barbara Hollander Lifetime Achievement Award from the Family Firm Institute. He has also been recognized with the Freedom Foundation's Leavey Award for Excellence in Private Enterprise Education and the William Hugh McEniry Award for Excellence in Teaching. He and the Family Enterprise Center at Stetson University have been honored nationally with the Irwin/McGraw Hill Innovation in Pedagogy Award. Stetson also received the U.S. Association for Small Business and Entrepreneurship's Model Program Award.

McCann is the author of *Who Do You Think You Are? Aligning Your Character and Reputation* and is the coauthor or editor of numerous books and journal articles. As one of the leading speakers and scholars in the field, McCann is often sought by the media as an expert source for articles on family business-related topics. McCann grew up working in his family business, held several positions at other companies, and was both a CPA and a lawyer.

90936730R00146

Made in the USA
Columbia, SC
12 March 2018